Writing Reviews

Lucy Calkins, Elizabeth Dunford,
Celena Dangler Larkey

Photography by Peter Cunningham

HEINEMANN ◆ PORTSMOUTH, NH

This book is dedicated to Jeff, for knowing I could before I even started. —Liz

This book is dedicated to Denny and Vada. Thank you for teaching me that every voice matters. —Celena

This book is dedicated in memory of Dawn, whose heroism on behalf of children illuminates the work that teachers and principals do every day. —Lucy

DEDICATED TO TEACHERS™

*first*hand
An imprint of Heinemann
361 Hanover Street
Portsmouth, NH 03801–3912
www.heinemann.com

Offices and agents throughout the world

The authors and publisher wish to thank those who have generously given permission to reprint borrowed material:

Review of "Beyblade: Metal Fusion" from timetoplaymag.com (http://www.timetoplaymag.com/toys/2029/hasbro/beyblade-metal-fusion/).Reprinted by permission of Litzky Public Relations.

Cataloging-in-Publication data is on file with the Library of Congress.

ISBN-13: 978-0-325-04726-3
ISBN-10: 0-325-04726-X

Production: Elizabeth Valway, David Stirling, and Abigail Heim
Cover and interior designs: Jenny Jensen Greenleaf
Series includes photographs by Peter Cunningham, Nadine Baldasare, Elizabeth Dunford, and Joseph Tan
Composition: Publishers' Design and Production Services, Inc.
Manufacturing: Steve Bernier

Printed in the United States of America on acid-free paper
17 16 15 14 13 ML 3 4 5

Acknowledgments

AS WE PUT THE FINISHING TOUCHES on this book, we are reeling from the news from Sandy Hook Elementary School. Those children whose lives were so abruptly, so senselessly ended were writers, their classroom was a flourishing writing workshop, and one of us—Liz—is the staff developer at that school. Even without that personal link, there isn't a teacher anywhere who isn't walking in the shoes of the teachers from that school, who isn't thinking, "This could have been my kids."

In the face of those horrible events, we are glad to be writing a book for first-graders of the world. How we hope that this book, this unit, will help you to go through your life knowing that it's important to speak out, to voice your opinions—and knowing that it is also important for those opinions to be based on thoughtful consideration, on close observation, and on detailed evidence.

This book is deeply steeped in a study of opinion/argument writing. Long before the Common Core State Standards were even a whiff of an idea, the Teachers College Reading and Writing Project had developed units of study in persuasive writing. We are especially grateful to Amanda Hartman, associate director of the Project, who leads the organization's work in primary writing, and to Sarah Picard Taylor, who captured some of the Project's work in her earlier book on this topic. We're grateful, too, to Mary Ehrenworth and Kelly Boland Hohne, each of whom has played an especially important role in the K–8 learning progression on opinion/argument writing.

The Teachers College Reading and Writing Project's work on this topic has been enriched by a think tank on argument writing that is sponsored by the Council of Chief School Officers and that has brought our organization into a collaboration with ETS and helped us access the thinking of Paul Deane, whose careful, deep research on argument writing has informed our teaching.

We've spent a lot of time making sure that the methods of teaching writing featured in these pages represent our very best knowledge. We've studied Webb's Depth of Knowledge and Danielson's frameworks, and we've refined our best thinking about minilessons, small-group work, performance assessments, and the like. For help in all of this, we thank Janet Steinberg, Monique Knight, Lauren Kolbeck, and Rebecca Cronin, especially. We are better writers because we rub shoulders with others who care about the craft of writing as much as we do. We are especially thankful to Sarah Weeks, author of many children's books, who teaches writing in the Literacy Specialist program at Teachers College.

The book benefited from an extraordinary team at Heinemann. We're grateful to Felicia O'Brien, who has cared as much as we do that this book be worthy of those who will teach it and who will learn from it, and to Teva Blair, whose sky-high standards, craftsmanship, and hard work played such an important role in the series. We're also thankful to Charles McQuillen, who will bring the series to teachers across the world.

Last, and most importantly, we're thankful to the hundreds of teachers who have helped us learn about teaching opinion writing to first-graders. The students and teachers at PS 5 in the Bronx and at Franklin Elementary School in Summit, New Jersey, have especially contributed to our knowledge and to this book. Their opinions, their words, and their insights live inside the pages of this book. Their voices are strong, clear, and oh-so-very important.

The class described in this unit is a composite class. We wrote the units this way to bring you both a wide array of wonderful, quirky, various children and also to illustrate for you the predictable (and unpredictable) situations and responses this unit has created in classrooms across the nation and world.

—Lucy, Celena, and Liz

Contents

BEND III   Writing Persuasive Book Reviews

Welcome to the Unit

THIS BOOK aims to bring opinion writing to first-graders—to kids who are beginning to lose their baby teeth, to ride two-wheelers. Opinion writing is the genre of the academy. Essays, editorials, and reviews are all examples of opinion writing. But in this unit, the goal is not to channel six-year-olds into writing what fourth-grade teachers sometimes refer to as "the hamburger essay," with a topic sentence (the top bun), supporting paragraphs (the meat), and a generic closing that matches the topic sentence (the bottom bun). Instead, you will help your first-graders appreciate the power and purposes of writing. You will help the children in your care grow up knowing that people sort, rank, categorize, explain, convince, persuade, argue, give in, change, and are changed. In this unit, you will teach the important academic work of opinion writing in ways that are exactly suited to six-year-olds.

The unit begins with you teaching students that writing can give them a way to make and defend important decisions, such as "Which is my best beanie baby? My best baseball cap? Action figure? Plastic horse? Which is second best? Which wins the booby prize for being the worst?" Whatever the item being assessed, children will learn to write their judgments and their reasons for those judgments and to organize their reasons and supply supporting details for those reasons. Eventually, children will use their skills at writing to make and defend judgments to write reviews of all sorts—restaurant reviews, movie reviews, book reviews.

The Common Core State Standards call for a new focus on opinion writing. They list opinion writing first of the three types of writing and have devoted time and space to explaining "The Special Place of Argument in the Standards," citing research showing that the ability to write arguments is essential to success in college and the workforce (CCSS, Appendix A, p. 24).

In first grade, the Common Core expectations for opinion writing suggest that students will compose opinion pieces in which they "introduce the topic or name the book they are writing about, state an opinion, supply a reason for the opinion, and provide some sense of closure" (CCSS W 1.1). No longer is there mention of dictating or drawing. Though illustrations will continue to be important to your young writers, by the time they leave you, they will be moving toward composing the bulk of their pieces through writing. In addition, your students are now expected to "introduce the topic they are writing about (or name the book), supply a reason for their opinion, and provide some sense of closure" (W 1.1). Your writers also need to offer a sense to readers that their piece has a purposeful ending. The Common Core calls this "some sense of closure," leaving what counts as an ending open to the interpretation of the reader. You are apt to feel that your students can do more than this, and you will see that this unit pushes students to exceed the expectations of the Common Core for first-graders and, in fact, to meet many of the standards for second-graders. Interestingly, the Common Core Appendix C of sample student writing does not include an opinion piece at the first-grade level. However, in the informative/explanatory writing sample, an all-about book on Spain, the Common Core notes that the student offers "some sense of closure" by ending the piece with the words "One day when I am a researcher I am going to go to Spain and write about it." (p. 11). Thus, the Common Core seems to view a final comment as one possibility for ending a piece with a sense of closure.

You will also want to keep the language standards in mind for first and second grade. There are five new expectations required of first-graders in demonstrating command of conventions of standard written English in addition to other language standards that address grammar, usage, and spelling. Students are expected to "capitalize dates and names of people" (L 1.2a), "use end punctuation for sentences" (L 1.2b), "use commas in dates and to separate single words in a series" (L 1.2c), "use conventional spelling for words with common spelling patterns and for frequently occurring irregular words" (L 1.2d), and "spell untaught words phonetically, drawing on phonemic awareness and spelling conventions" (L 1.2e). It is worth talking to your colleagues who teach kindergarten about editing checklists, charts, and so on, helping those teachers create tools to remind students of what they *already* should know how to do (e.g., capitalize the first word in a sentence, capitalize the pronoun *I*).

You may feel that your students can do more than what the standards expect, and you will, of course, teach to high standards for your students. We agree with you that first-graders can often do more than the standards require, and you will see that this unit pushes students to exceed the standards. As you assess your students' writing, you may see evidence of meeting and exceeding first-grade language and conventions standards, and we highly suspect you will by this time of the year. With that in mind, however, you will want to first make sure that your students understand what the standards expect of them and can do this work well before you move them to outgrow it. The important work that they do this year will directly prepare them for what they will encounter in the future. This unit reaches beyond grade 1 standards, both in the teaching of opinion writing (where there are sessions modeling and encouraging writers to develop opinions with multiple reasons and provide detailed descriptions), as well as language and convention sessions focused on students constructing and revising complex sentences (CCSS 2.1.f). Next year in second-grade opinion writing, they'll be expected to supply multiple reasons, use linking words, and provide a more formal concluding statement or section.

OVERVIEW OF THE UNIT

The first portion of the unit is built on the notion that six-year-olds collect stuff. Go for a walk with a six-year-old. It can be through the woods or along the beach—it doesn't matter. When you arrive home, the youngster's pockets will be full—a few acorns (looking like elves) and two rocks, one with veins of gold running through it, the other bearing the faint impress of a fern. Or dig through the child's backpack, lunch box, or cubby. You'll find a collection of stickers or bracelets, trolls or baseball cards.

If you think about it, the stuff that a person collects is the grist for that person's writing mill. In the first session, you'll create a glorified show-and-tell session, but this time, instead of asking children to bring one robot, one

baseball cap, or one Barbie to school, you'll ask each child to bring a small collection, with the collection stored neatly in a shoebox. Once children have collections in hand, instead of following the traditional show-and-tell format in which each child takes his or her seat, in sequence, at the front of the room and then talks (on and on) about whatever that child wants to share, children will instead use writing to think and "talk" about the stuff of their lives. Specifically, they will learn to review their collections and to make choices about which item in that collection is the best, writing defenses for those judgments. This writing will become their introduction to writing reviews, the subject of this book. It will also help children to grow up realizing that writing is a way to wrap their mental arms around the topics and causes and objects and obsessions that define them, and in doing so, to grow opinions and insights about all that matters most to them.

During the second bend in the path of this unit, students will write review after review, writing these about anything and everything: toys, restaurants, video games, the works. You might involve your students in reviews on restaurants, books, or kid-friendly places to play.

The bend supports revision as well as qualities of good writing, and it highlights independence. Students study mentor texts, and now their writing will begin to look like what you would expect to see in persuasive writing. You'll look for the essentials—claims or opinions, followed by reasons and explanations of those reasons. Then you can look for other qualities of effective writing mentioned in the unit checklist.

Meanwhile, you will strongly remind students that they already know that writers revise. Because your minilessons will often involve teaching a new quality of good persuasive writing, you should see your writers going back to previous reviews, rereading to judge whether they incorporated the new quality they just learned about in that review and then revising to do that. On any one day, some children will be revising previously written reviews and some will be writing new ones. Keep an eye on volume and be prepared to set clear expectations and to plan for extra time during the day for children to make up the missed work if they haven't produced at least six lengthy reviews each by the end of ten days or so of work within this unit.

You'll look also for children's willingness to edit and their particular needs. Note what they can do without help, and think about how you can help different groups of your children progress in this arena. If some are not using commas in lists, for example, you can teach that now. If some are not rereading for meaning, noticing when their writing makes no sense or is overly repetitive, you can do some small-group work to support that language structure work.

Toward the end of this bend, students can gather their reviews and begin to create anthologies, such as a mini-kid-version *Zagat* guide to restaurants or a collection of book reviews or a collection of another type of similar reviews.

Finally, in Bend III, children will learn to write book reviews. They'll summarize, evaluate, judge, and defend their judgments. You'll take the best parts of the first two bends of the unit—collection writing and review structure—and weave them together to support children writing book reviews. From the first bend of the unit, you will teach children that much like they collected things and judged those things, they can collect and judge books, then write to tell others their opinions about those books. From the second bend, you'll return to teaching your children how to write to persuade, using all they've learned about review structure and persuasive writing. You'll return to the different kinds of writing with which you launched the unit, asking writers to work on individual projects that convince others to read and be interested in the books they are reading. The unit ends in a big, old-fashioned celebration teaching children to speak to others about their books and persuade others to read their books, much like the *Reading Rainbow* book reviews of years past from PBS.

ASSESSMENT

We recognize that the first-graders entering your classroom will bring a wide range of skills. Some will still be fledgling writers, while others will be ready for anything you put before them. Your teaching will need to be especially assessment-based and designed to support this diversity.

Hopefully long before this unit, you will already have conducted on-demand assessments of your students' abilities to write in the three genres—narrative, opinion, and information—and have been using the data as a way to plan your instruction. You will absolutely want to reassess your children's opinion writing just prior to this unit, and just after it as well. Devote one writing period to this assessment, giving children forty-five minutes of actual writing time (and there will be more time for you to set them up, get them started, and so forth). Be sure kids have four-page booklets in which to write, with at least five lines per page. Then allow students to write on their own, doing the best work they can do.

Before you administer any assessment, we recommend that you and your grade level colleagues meet to be sure that you are in absolute agreement on any way you might deviate from the protocol detailed in *Writing Pathways: Performance Assessments and Learning Progressions, K–5*. You want to be clear that the teachers across first grade all convey the directions and expectations to your individual classes in the same way so that when it comes time to compare data across the grade, you will know that the circumstances under which the assessment was administered and taken were identical.

A word of caution: for this initial assessment to provide accurate baseline data on your writers' opinion writing skills, it is essential that you not scaffold your students' work during this assessment. Think of it this way: the worse they do, the more dramatic their progress across the unit will be! You'll want to simply read them the prompt and the descriptors of what is expected (see below), then step back and leave them to their own devices. We recommend that you give students the following prompt to start them off.

> "Think of a topic or issue that you know and care about, an issue about which you have strong feelings. Tomorrow, you will have forty-five minutes to write an opinion or argument text in which you will write your opinion or claim and tell reasons why you feel that way. When you do this, draw on everything you know about essays, persuasive letters, and reviews. If you want to find and use information from a book or another outside source, you may bring that with you tomorrow. Please keep in mind that you'll have forty-five minutes to complete this, so you will need to plan, draft, revise, and edit in one sitting."

We suggest that students be in their regular writing seats, with familiar paper on hand (and a supply of additional pages for any who might want to write more) when you tell them the prompt and show them the chart of suggestions.

Once you have collected students' on-demand work, use the Opinion/Argument Learning Progression and exemplar pieces to ascertain the level of work that students are doing early in this unit, and then track their progress over its course and beyond, throughout the year. The learning progressions for narrative, information, and opinion writing (along with the checklists) are available in *Writing Pathways: Performance Assessments and Learning Progressions, K–5*. These three learning progressions are closely aligned to the Common Core State Standards and are designed to support teachers in assessing writing skill development and creating teaching points.

They will also help you see where, in the trajectory of writing development, each of your students lies. By studying the learning progressions and on-demand assessment pieces together, you and each student will be able to identify next steps for his or her progress. Children will also see the ways they have improved across the unit, and you'll have something concrete to share with their parents at parent-teacher conferences. There's nothing like being able to say, "Look at how your child has grown! At the start of the unit (or year), she was doing . . . and now she's doing . . . !"

Many teachers have found it helpful to give children a copy of their on-demand assessment piece to tape to the front of their writer's notebook. This piece can then serve as a reminder to the writer and to you that this was the level of work that he or she produced at the start of the unit. Having the on-demand writing close on hand will hold writers accountable to producing increasingly stronger work as the unit progresses. You may need to remind students to revisit that first piece occasionally, as a point of comparison.

Of course, in addition to assessing where each individual child in your class falls along the Opinion/Argument Writing Learning Progression, you will also want to assess where the bulk of your class falls, letting that information inform the upcoming unit of study. You can compare each student's draft to the exemplar texts and then read the descriptors at that level of the learning progression to determine specific ways that each child can improve. As you do this, bear in mind that no text will match a checklist in its entirety; you can use the rubric for the grade level to determine whether a piece of writing that generally matches the first-grade level (or the second-grade level) with a few exceptions can be assessed as on-grade-level. The descriptors can help you provide the child with specific next steps that he or she can take to strengthen the writing. You can tell a child whose opinion work straddles level 1 to look at the descriptors for, say, structure for level 2 and note whether it seems the writing could soon adhere to those. If so, tell that child, or your whole class, if this is broadly applicable, "You used to structure your piece by . . . ," and read the descriptors from level K, "but now you are . . . ," and read the descriptor for level 1. Then say, "Here's a pointer to make your writing even better! You can . . . ," and read from the level 2 descriptor. You can even say, "Let me show you an example," and then cite a section of the level 2 exemplar text.

One final word. The baseline assessment at the start of the unit is designed to assess the knowledge base of this particular genre that your students bring with them. But this initial assessment, studied side by side the exact same one you will administer at the unit's end, tells a much bigger story. It can show you not only how your students have grown across a unit and across a year, but also how your teaching and this curriculum have worked, too. The goal of any writing instruction is not only to produce strong writing. It is to produce strong writers and strong writing instruction, too. As you review your students' initial assessments, then, don't think simply about how to teach into this one piece of writing on this one day, but into any piece of writing on any day. That is, you'll use the assessments to think about lines of growth—for your students and for yourself as a teacher—and the exciting thing is, we know that when you look across your assessments at the end of this year, you'll see progress.

GETTING READY

To get the students warmed up for opinion writing, you might immerse them in persuasion. You might read them mentor texts that have strong persuasive voices—books like *Earrings* by Judith Viorst, the *Pigeon* books by Mo Willems, or *A Pet for Petunia* by Paul Schmid. Steep your students in the sound of persuasion and let them listen for how the characters in these books try to convince others.

In addition to the books you'll chose to read and share with your first-graders, you may decide to engage students in whole-class testing and opinion forming. Perhaps you'll bring in a trio of fruits or gummy candies and let the children taste them, rank them, and talk about favorites and reasons why.

You might even prepare students for the unit by giving them the opportunity to take positions and have conversations and debates about topics and texts. You might start off by providing two different positions and letting your students choose one. "Some people say cats are a better pet than dogs," you might announce, pointing to one side of your room. "Others say dogs are a better pet than cats," you can continue, indicating the other side of the room. "Choose your position and stand on the side of the room that matches what you think!" Encourage children to take a position, no matter what. You might decide to do a few "taking a position" activities, letting your students get the sense of what it feels like to stand up and make a clear choice. Or you might move your students toward having a quick debate. You might have each side of the room form a line and have your children meet in the middle, each one facing his or her "opponent." After children who will debate each other shake hands, you might give each "position team" time to talk and come up with reasons why their chosen pet is the better choice. Then your children can meet in partnerships, each partnership made of one child from each side of the debate. They can take turns each laying out the reasons for their position and then have time to talk back to each other. You can even move students from having these debates over real-world topics to text-based debates, where they might take a position on your class read-aloud. "Some people say the character Junie B. Jones is a brat," you might announce. "Position A—you agree. Position B—you disagree." And the debating process can start again, this time with children considering the text to defend their thinking.

This warm-up work can take place across the curriculum. Perhaps during your morning meeting, you can incorporate class questions such as "Should all classrooms have pets? Should the cafeteria serve pizza twice a week?" You can break out the Post-its® and let students decide. "Yes? No? Maybe?" You can even take these Post-its to math workshop and give your students a chance to exercise their math skills by involving them in counting, tallying, and making quick graphs of the responses of the class. Early forms of argument can become a way of life in your room, rallying your students for the unit ahead and preparing them for the work they will encounter in future years.

People Collect Things and Write Opinions about Their Collections

IN THIS SESSION, you'll teach students that when writers care a lot about something—dogs, hats, T-shirts, superhero figures—they often collect examples of that topic, and then spend time judging all they have collected, thinking, "This is the best because . . ." They try to convince others of their opinions.

GETTING READY

✔ Student writing folders, emptied of all previous writing, which has been sent home, filed, or published

✔ Each child's shoebox collection of his or her favorite things

✔ Your own shoebox collection. This will thread through the unit. I use a collection of five plastic dogs. More would not be better! (see Teaching)

✔ Chart paper with prewritten heading, "To Judge Fairly" written at the top, markers, clipboards, and a judge's hat (see Active Engagement)

✔ Stacks of First Place Blue Ribbon paper at each table as well as a fully stocked writing center (see Mid-Workshop Teaching)

✔ Post-it® notes of varying colors (see Share)

COMMON CORE STATE STANDARDS: W.1.1, W.2.1, RI.1.8, SL.1.1, SL.1.4, L.1.1, L.1.2, L.1.5.a

SIX-YEAR-OLDS COLLECT STUFF. Go for a walk with a six-year-old—it can be through the woods or along the beach, it doesn't matter. When you arrive home, the youngster's pockets will be full—a few acorns (looking like elves) and two rocks, one with veins of gold running through it, the other bearing the faint impress of a fern. Or dig through the child's backpack, lunch box, or cubby. You'll find a collection of stickers or bracelets, trolls or baseball cards.

If you think about it, the stuff that a person collects is the grist for that person's writing mill. After all, Celena, Liz, and I collect writing by young children and stories from heroic teachers. And then, when we sit down to write, we spin all that we have collected into sentences, chapters, proposals, speeches, books. Do children know that they can do the same?

In this session, you create a glorified show-and-tell session, but this time, instead of asking children to bring one robot, one baseball cap, or one Barbie to school, you ask each child to bring a small collection, with the collection stored neatly into a shoebox. Some children may forget or may claim to have no collections, in which case they can easily make collections of beloved books from the classroom library. Or with just a pen and some index cards, they can make a collection of favorite movie titles or favorite toys, favorite songs, or favorite places. Have on hand empty shoeboxes for children who need to gather and create a collection in class, along with spare collection items, such as books, photographs of animals, or plastic creatures. Once children have collections in hand, instead of following the traditional show-and-tell format in which each child takes his or her seat, in sequence, at the front of the room and then talks (on and on) about whatever that child wants to share, you can teach children that they can use writing to think and "talk" about the stuff of their lives. You will be teaching them not only to build on their interests and follow their passions—an important life lesson—but also to use writing to form, convey, and support their opinions.

If you wonder how this session fits with the announced topic of *Writing Reviews*—know that the progression is that children learn to evaluate, to rank, first the items in

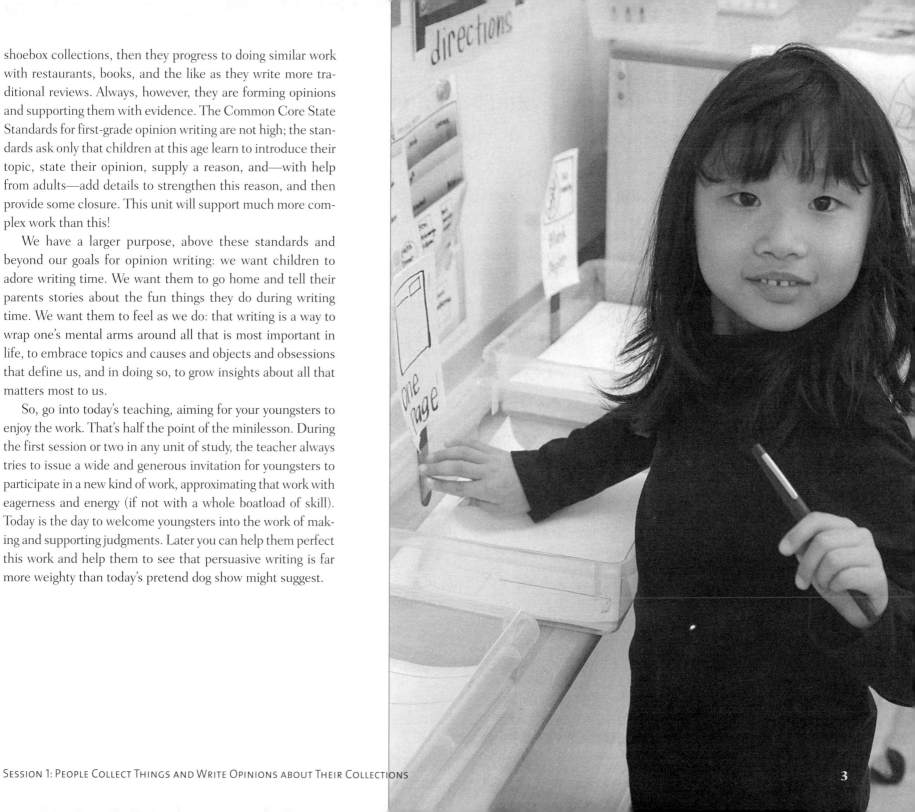

shoebox collections, then they progress to doing similar work with restaurants, books, and the like as they write more traditional reviews. Always, however, they are forming opinions and supporting them with evidence. The Common Core State Standards for first-grade opinion writing are not high; the standards ask only that children at this age learn to introduce their topic, state their opinion, supply a reason, and—with help from adults—add details to strengthen this reason, and then provide some closure. This unit will support much more complex work than this!

We have a larger purpose, above these standards and beyond our goals for opinion writing: we want children to adore writing time. We want them to go home and tell their parents stories about the fun things they do during writing time. We want them to feel as we do: that writing is a way to wrap one's mental arms around all that is most important in life, to embrace topics and causes and objects and obsessions that define us, and in doing so, to grow insights about all that matters most to us.

So, go into today's teaching, aiming for your youngsters to enjoy the work. That's half the point of the minilesson. During the first session or two in any unit of study, the teacher always tries to issue a wide and generous invitation for youngsters to participate in a new kind of work, approximating that work with eagerness and energy (if not with a whole boatload of skill). Today is the day to welcome youngsters into the work of making and supporting judgments. Later you can help them perfect this work and help them to see that persuasive writing is far more weighty than today's pretend dog show might suggest.

People Collect Things and Write Opinions about Their Collections

CONNECTION

Explain that people use writing to think about stuff and to get others to think about stuff as well—the stuff might be a collection.

"Writers, we've often talked about how kids use writing to do things: to tell stories, to teach people. Today we're starting a new unit, and in this unit, you will use writing to form opinions about stuff . . . *and* to persuade other people to share those opinions. Do you remember that last year, you studied ways to get readers to share your opinions about problems in your class and in the world? You wrote things like, 'It is bad when people run in the halls,' or 'People should not pollute.' Well, this year, you'll be convincing people to think as you do about *stuff*.

"So I brought a collection of stuff in my shoebox. How many of you remembered to bring a collection in your shoebox?" Most children signaled that yes, they'd brought a small collection. "If you don't have a shoebox full of something—stickers, rubber Ninjas, baseball cards, hair bands, Lego guys—you can later get some favorite books or pens or math manipulatives and make yourself a collection right after our minilesson," I said. "Or you could make a list of favorite places, or songs, or whatever you want."

❖ Name the teaching point.

"Today I want to teach you that people who know a lot about something—like people who keep collections—often think, 'Which is my favorite? Which is next?' And people write and talk to tell others about their opinions. They even try to *convince* others about their opinions."

◆ COACHING

One of the challenges in devising a K–8 curriculum is that it is important not only to convey that one unit is unique and different from the rest but also that the skills one learned earlier are skills that are meant to be used and built upon for a lifetime. This unit stands on the shoulders of the Persuasive Writing of All Kinds *unit in kindergarten and yet approaches opinion writing from quite a different trajectory.*

Minilessons are a form of oral instruction. We write them down to share them, but they live as spoken language. I find that the best minilessons have an informal, intimate, spoken-language quality. Whenever helping teachers write minilessons, I suggest they avoid writing them at the computer and, instead, write them by talking and then jotting with a pen on paper, old-fashioned style. This helps to make the minilessons feel more homespun, more oral.

TEACHING

Show children your collection (mine is of rubber dogs, of many breeds), and recruit them to join you in judging your collection (in my instance, creating a dog show).

"In a few minutes, you are going to have a chance to do what people do—to think about the things you know about, that you collect, and then to write some of your opinions. But first, do you mind helping me to think about my collection?"

From my shoebox, I produced five toy dogs. "Have any of you ever watched a dog show, either in real life or on television? A judge with a clipboard inspects each dog. He checks the shape of the dog's head, feels its fur, and looks into its eyes. Then he says, 'Walk your dog' and he watches the dog walk in a circle. After a while the judge will announce, 'Ladies and gentlemen, we have our winners. In first place . . .' and he will announce the winner. Later, he'll have a bunch of reasons for why that dog was more special than the others."

Explain that in this unit, they'll be judging not just dogs but items in their own collections, and movies, books, and restaurants.

"I'm telling you this because what that judge does—deciding which dog is the best and giving his or her reasons—is something you will do a lot in this unit. You can help me be a judge for my dogs, and you can be a judge for your own collection—of Lego guys, hair bands, stickers, baseball cards, and the like. Later on in this unit, you'll also be the judge for restaurants, TV shows, movies, and books."

ACTIVE ENGAGEMENT

Recruit a volunteer judge. Role-play what not to do, contrasting that with a list of what responsible judges should do. Channel the judge to weigh one trait at a time, across contenders.

"For now, let's learn some things about being a good judge by judging my collection of dogs. I need a volunteer to be our dog show judge, and we'll all notice what you do to judge and see if we can think about what a really serious, really fair, judge should do. 'Cause would it be okay if I judged the dog show like this?" I glanced at the dogs, threw my hands up in a "whatever?" gesture, and flicked a finger at one dog and said, "He's the best. I don't know why, just 'cause . . ." Shifting out of the role of a cavalier judge, I asked the children, "Would *that* be what you'd expect of a dog show judge?"

On cue, the children chimed, "No . . ." and one came to the front of the room to role-play being a judge. I gave Bradley a clipboard and a hat. I put the dogs in a line for him and channeled him to look closely at the first one, then at the next one.

"Writers, will you talk quietly with each other, naming what you see Bradley doing that seems like wise judging?" Children articulated what they saw Bradley doing, and Bradley continued his judging. I whispered to Bradley that it would

By now, you will have seen that an enormous love for dogs winds in and out of these books. There is nothing essential about bringing dogs into your teaching, but your teaching will be more intense and intimate if you bring whatever you love to it. If you adore owls and have owl coffee cups and owl doormats in your house, your kids want to know that, and they'll want to help you assess whether the screech owl is better or worse looking than the barn owl. The fact that dogs thread in and out of these minilessons should signal that you need to bring your life to your teaching.

When acting the "what not to do" part, always exaggerate to bring home the point and give kids some fun.

Keep your eye on the clock. Kids do not need to see one child weighing the pros and cons of a beagle versus a German shepherd for very long! Make sure your judge moves along quickly and gets through this without going into excessive detail.

help if he looked into each dog's eyes, one by one, and thought which had the best eyes. As he did this, I inquired, in a voice all the children could hear, "So, Bradley, are you looking into each dog's eyes? Is that the plan? To look at the same thing—like for now, the eyes—on each of your dogs?" Again, I asked children to tell each other what they noticed the judge was doing that they could do when it was their turn to judge their collections.

As the students shared their ideas with partners about what they noticed the judge was doing, I quickly jotted what I had overheard on a piece of chart paper.

> ### To Judge Fairly
>
> 1. Put everything in a line.
> 2. Compare the same thing (eyes, fur, and so on) on each, thinking, "Which has the best . . . ?"

Channel all children to function as judges for your collection, reminding them how a judge goes about making fair decisions and leading them to choose the winner and to provide reasons.

"Let's each try being the judge at this dog show. I'll pass the dogs around so that you can look at each one closely (but quickly, please). Remember to look at the same thing on each dog. How about if for now, you look at the fur on each dog and assess it?" Then the dogs were paraded in front of all the judges. As they examined them, I said, "Be thinking which is first place, and why. How will you explain your decision?"

After the dogs had circulated, I said, "So, judges. Make your decision. Which dog is number one, and why? Tell your opinion and your reasons to your partner."

Ask one individual to report and defend his or her "Best in Show" choice, coaching into the one child's work in ways that help that child to elaborate.

Once I'd called for the class's attention, I asked for volunteers to announce their "Best in Show" choices and the reasons behind those choices. Thomas's hand shot up, and when I called on him, he scrambled to his feet, collected the collie from the pile of dogs, and held it high. "This guy is the best, the number one."

I said, "Thomas, do you think that is enough for a judge to say 'This is the best'? Or do you think a judge needs to give his reasons?" Thomas looked at the dog in his hand, his finger rubbing gently over the back of the little rubber dog, then he held the dog up for the class to see and said, "His fur is good! This dog has all different colors of fur."

"Go on," I nudged as the room buzzed a bit with children who were murmuring their agreement, while others were shaking their heads, eager to share their choice and their opinions. "Say, 'Another thing . . .'"

Again, you really need to watch the time. You may just hold each dog up and "walk" it in front of the class. Don't let more than five compete!

Notice that when I ask, "Do you think it is enough for a judge to say 'This is the best' or do you think the judge needs to give reasons," I am not just saying, "Thomas, will you explain why you like this dog's fur the best?" The way that I word my coaching makes it applicable—transferable—to another day, another instance of judging, whereas if I'd simply asked a situation-specific question such as, "Why do you like this dog's fur the best?" that is not as transferable.

"Another thing I really like about this dog that makes him my most favorite, is that his ears have tufts of fur coming out of them," Thomas said, again holding the dog up, with his fingers touching the tufts on the dog's ears.

Unpack, out loud, the reasons and details in the child's opinion in ways that help the rest of the children support their own choices.

"Whoa," I said. "Look at how Thomas explained his opinion! The reason he awarded this one 'Best in Show' is that this dog's fur is the best. And he gave details: this one has the most *different* colors in his fur. Some of you might have picked a different dog and decided it had the best fur for a different reason, like maybe you picked a dog because its fur was the softest. But Thomas gave his own reasons!

"Thomas gave another detail to support his judgment of the dog's fur—he said this dog's ears have tufts of hair coming from them. Thomas didn't just say, 'It's my favorite, it's the best,' and leave it at that. No way! He went on. He gave reasons and details. He said, 'This dog is my favorite *because* of his fur. It is colorful, and there are tufts of it in his ears.' We should add what Thomas did to our list of how to judge fairly." I added one final bullet:

> 3. Decide which is the best and give reasons. Say "BECAUSE . . ."

LINK

Send children off to judge their own collections similarly, writing about the item they like best and their reasons for this judgment.

"I know you want to judge your own collections. Although you have heard of dog shows, you may not have heard of hair band shows, or Lego shows, but the truth is, people who have collections do think, 'Which is my favorite, next favorite, and why?'" I reminded children of our chart containing a list of ways to judge fairly.

"Writers often rank whatever it is they know about—sports teams, songs, outfits—deciding which is the best and saying why, and then offering up opinions. Use what you have learned about judging fairly to think about the items in your own collection and decide on your own opinions, then write reasons for your opinion. Later, when you put one of your things in the winner's circle, you can put your writing beside your choice.

"The kind of writing you will be doing is called opinion writing, and for this unit of study, you will learn to do it really, really well. In your whole, entire life, whenever you are writing an opinion, you will always need to explain your reasons, just like you are doing today. Okay, who is ready for a Lego show, a hat show, a car show? If you are ready, 'Judges on duty!' Off you go!"

Be aware that there are an armload of ways you can name what this one child has done. He has supplied evidence. He has substantiated his opinion. He has said more. He has elaborated. He has given examples. He has included details. I try to not name one action by ten different names—a different name each time I discuss the concept—but instead select the label that I'll use for this particular action and use that one label repeatedly for a long while. Only once the kids have a firm grasp of the concept will I provide a synonym or two, and at that point, I'll use both the now-familiar term and the new one.

Teachers, you will want to decide how much you want to emphasize the "Best in Show" metaphor, with the winner's circle and the accompanying blue ribbon, and how much you want to let go of that particular spin on the process of reviewing and judging and forming opinions. The kids will probably enjoy it as you play up the competitive angle, using terms like "Best in Show," but this work is more transferable to what writers do if you downplay that a bit and instead talk about the fact that they're reviewing and supporting opinions.

Again, you can decide to tone down the "Judges on duty!" talk and instead send kids off to review all the items in their collection, determine which they think is especially good, and decide upon their reasons.

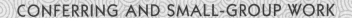

Launching the Work by Supporting Thoughtful Evaluations

DURING THE FIRST DAY OF MANY UNITS OF STUDY, you'll want to circulate extra quickly to make sure that all of your children grasp what is being asked of them and are able to get engaged in the work, even if the details of what they are doing are not yet perfect. So instead of hovering with one child, luring that child to provide more elaborated reasons and to use more domain-specific vocabulary to describe his or her reasons, you'll probably accept more approximations than usual and mostly channel students into throwing themselves head over heels into this work.

The best way to recruit children to care about the work is for you to care about it as well. So as you move from one child to another, one collection to another, take the job of judging these collections seriously. Remember that although the little furry trolls in one child's box may not be your cup of tea, those trolls are as important to that collector as a collection of your students' drafts are to you. You'll find that if you approach children's collections with enormous interest and recruit children to tell you the criteria they use to assess their items, you'll put children in positions of expertise and help them to talk with authority about their collections. This, of course, will set them up to engage in exactly the kind of writing that you hope they do.

Although it can take just seconds to rank items from best to worst, this sort of work can also require a lot of thought. Your first goal will be to help children take their roles as judges seriously. Certainly children will need to be reminded that a judge looks at each entrant with one lens in mind, then looks at each entrant with another lens, and another. As the judge does this work, he or she is essentially thinking, "What makes this better or worse?" That is, what makes one dog's eyes rank better than another dog's eyes? Some children will be apt to shrug and say, "I dunno. I just liked it better," in which case you will absolutely want to teach children that being able to talk and think about qualities is essential, as is being able to cite evidence. Any judge needs to substantiate his or her opinions with evidence. Furthermore, it is helpful to not just point to the evidence but to discuss it, to "unpack" it. Why does fur that contains more color rate better than fur of just one color?

MID-WORKSHOP TEACHING
Help Children Imagine Forms for Their Opinion Writing

"Writers, can I have your attention for just one minute?" Once all eyes were on me, I continued on. "Writers, some of you are wondering what this kind of writing looks like. What paper do you use? I've put a pile of paper, each containing a first-place blue ribbon and lots of space for you to write the reasons for your choice, on your tables. But you can also invent other ways that your writing can go. You could decide to write a whole book that is just about all the reasons that your first-place dog or kind of candy or book is so special. On every page you could write, 'It is special because . . .' and tell another reason. Or one page can be on the first-place dog or hair band, with the next page being for the second-place. These decisions are up to you because you are the author. There are paper choices in the writing center, if you decide to use paper other than the kind at the center of your tables."

As Students Continue Working . . .

"Oh, my goodness. Ashley just came up with a new idea that some of you might try as well. She is giving out red ribbons as well as blue ones! Red ribbons are for things that come in second place. Great idea, Ashley."

Of course, part and parcel of helping children take their judging seriously will be helping children move from looking at and talking about the items in their collections toward writing about them.

As I sat down beside Rosa, I noticed she had sketched quick pictures of her opinions, choosing the orange cat in her collection as her favorite, and had also added details by awarding "second and third places" with numbers and labels (see Figure 1–1). After I studied her work for a moment, I began. "Hi, Rosa. Tell me about the work you're planning to do as a writer today."

Orange fluffy kitten, you are the winner! You are fluffy. Even fluffier than the black kitten. Winner! Winner! Winner! Fluffy! Fluffy! Fluffy!

Rosa paused in her writing and looked up at me. "I'm going to tell about my orange cat because I like him best. I drew my most favorite and the other two that I like."

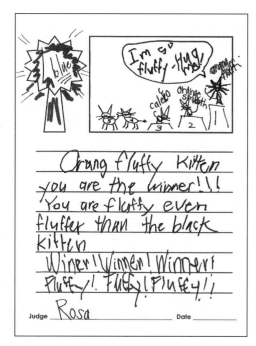

FIG. 1–1   Rosa is more clear as to which is her favorite than why.

I wanted to name for Rosa the work she was planning on doing, so that it would be clear to her that her strategy was transferable to other days, other pieces. Also, summarizing what a student tells me signifies to them that I am listening to what it is they are telling me. Their words are important. "So, Rosa, let me make sure I understand what you are planning to do today during workshop. You're planning to write a piece that tells your opinion about the cats in your collection. You looked at all the cats in your collection," I said, gesturing to the first step on the "How to Judge Fairly" chart, "then you compared the same thing on each?"

I paused for a moment and Rosa said, "Yeah. I looked at fur. I like the orange cat. It has fluff."

"Wow, you have big plans ahead of you. So, tell me, how's it going to sound when you write the rest of your opinion about the orange cat? Like, what are you going to put on the next page?" I wanted to push Rosa to imagine that she could extend her writing.

"I'm going to write that the orange kitten is the winner because it is the fluffiest," Rosa said, as she pointed to the picture. "It's fluffiest and cute."

I said, "What other ways did you compare the orange kitten to the others in your collection?" Rosa stared at me, then looked back to her paper. "It's fluffier than the black kitten," she added.

"Rosa, you're definitely thinking like an opinion writer. Just like in the newspaper, when opinion writers write and share their thinking and choices, they tell what their opinion is so that the readers know their thinking. I want to remind you that as you write your opinion, you want to be sure to add a couple reasons that tell *why* it is your favorite. Look at step three on the chart," I said, and pointed to the chart still sitting on the easel. "You've told one reason—the fluffy fur—but you need to judge more than one trait. Consider personality or size or shape or eyes . . . then write 'because . . .' and tell more reasons. That helps your readers to understand your opinion."

Rosa looked solemnly at me and nodded her head. Before I left this conference, I took the opportunity to reiterate the writing strategy, stressing the importance of it being applicable to all opinion writing. As you write other opinion pieces this week, and next week, and from now on—keep doing that hard work of lining up all the choices, then comparing one to the others, and then writing several reasons why you chose the one you did. You'll use the word *because* to help explain your thinking.

Developing Systems to Organize Your Judgments

Teach the class the way one child developed a system for assessing one trait (on one color Post-it note) and then another trait, helping to solidify the trait-based assessment.

"Kids, I want to show you what Alejandro figured out to help him with picking the best in his matchbox car show! I asked Alejandro to set up right here on the top of this bookcase so you could see. What he did was this: he lined up all his cars. Then, he decided to use *blue* Post-it notes to judge the speeds at which each of his cars travel. So after putting a blue note in front of each car, he then wrote that car's speed on that paper. Look, he wrote 'terrible' speed on this one and drew just two stars. Meanwhile he wrote 'so-so' on some others, with four or five stars, and he wrote 'super super fast' on this one, with ten stars.

"He didn't just judge his cars' speeds. He also judged the cars' prices. On a *yellow* Post-it note, he wrote the price of any car he could remember, and he circled the most expensive car as the winner of that category.

"Do you see how this system works? Alejandro is using a different-color Post-it note for each quality that he is judging and making notes that capture his opinion on that quality—speed and price.

"Will you turn to your partner and talk about what the traits were that you used to judge the items in your collection? If you didn't have a system like Alejandro's, talk about whether that sort of a system could work for you."

Explaining Judgments in Convincing Ways

MANY OF THE ADULTS IN A SCHOOL never received the writing education that you are giving to your students. If you and your colleagues talk about the writing education that you each received, you will probably find that most of your colleagues usually wrote one draft only and then turned in that piece of writing for comments from the teacher. The paper would be returned with notes like "awk" or "details!" written in the margin and with no expectation that the writer would do something with that draft. If ever a writer was asked to redo a piece of writing, it was because the initial draft was really below par. Most adults in a school were brought up to believe that revision was punishment for writing that didn't make the mark.

It is a big deal that today, Day Two of this exciting unit, is a day for revision. Your children are growing up expecting that first-draft writing will almost always require revision, and they are being taught that revision is no big deal. Earlier this year, during their information writing unit, whenever they learned a new quality of effective information writing, they used that new quality both as they wrote their upcoming chapter and also as a lens for rereading and reconsidering all their so-called finished chapters. Writing was a process of "one step forward, one step backward." Today, you let writers know that this unit will be no different.

Prior to today, the children will probably have written several pages about the items in their collections that they like best and next best. It would be interesting to ask a few children, before today's class, "What do you think you'll be learning about and doing in today's writing workshop?" Your hope is that by now, your children have internalized the rhythm of writing, then rereading one's writing with an eye toward particular qualities of good writing, and revising that writing to improve upon it.

You, as well, should have internalized this rhythm. You should find yourself anticipating how units unfold, because soon the support you've been given for these four units of study will fall away, and you'll be left to hopefully design your own units. So notice that Day One, you issue a generous invitation, getting writers to write up a storm, and Day Two (or Three), you teach qualities of whatever kind of writing the children are doing

IN THIS SESSION, you'll teach students that when writing about their opinions, writers need to give several reasons and provide supporting details for these reasons.

GETTING READY

✔ Students need to bring the shoebox collections to the minilesson (see Connection)

✔ Chart paper and marker to create "Convince Your Reader!" chart (see Teaching)

✔ Your own shoebox collection (see Active Engagement)

✔ An object that serves as microphone (it could be anything from a Mr. Microphone to your fist and thumb) to role-play being judges (see Active Engagement)

✔ Half-sheets of paper, tape, revision strips, Post-it notes, colored pens, and staplers set out on tables (see Link)

✔ Ribbon paper choice (see Mid-Workshop Teaching)

COMMON CORE STATE STANDARDS: W.1.1, W.1.5, W.2.1, RI.1.8, SL.1.1, SL.1.2, SL.1.4, L.1.1.g, L.1.2

and encourage children to reread and revise so as to bring out those qualities. Start with the most accessible qualities and the ones that seem most needed. Opinion writers write with lots of reasons, not just one, and they support those reasons with detailed, specific observations, not just with generalities.

"Opinion writers write with lots of reasons, not just one, and they support those reasons with detailed, specific observations, not just with generalities."

Any lesson on a quality of writing will require instruction in strategies as well as qualities. You can think of the qualities as the goal, and the strategies as the process for reaching the goal. In this instance, the focus is more on strategies for revising—use tape to add on a half-sheet of paper—than on ways to think of additional reasons, because we figure that making writing seem malleable is especially essential.

Explaining Judgments in Convincing Ways

CONNECTION

Ask children to show off the item they are writing opinions about, and help them remember their reasons for their opinion by talking to their partner.

"Writers, right now will you get out your 'Best in Show'? Your best hair band or best baseball card . . ." For a moment, everyone dug through their shoeboxes, pulling forth one item or another. "So hold your 'Best in Show' high," I said, and the children waved their items overhead.

"Partner 2, pretend someone with a TV camera wanted to know what *you'd* chosen for your 'Best in Show.' They've just passed you an imaginary microphone and asked you to explain to all the people watching your TV show (really, to Partner 1) why you selected *this* winner as your 'Best in Show.' Talk as if you are the judge, explaining your choice. Go!"

The children made their explanations, speaking into imaginary microphones to support their choices. Henry said, "This car is the fastest" into his microphone.

Before I could signal with a rolling hand that he could continue to provide more reasons, he held his hand "microphone" in front of Monique's mouth, nudging her to take a turn. Monique held up her purple foil candy wrapper from a long-ago-eaten chocolate egg and said into the imaginary mike, "This wrapper is the best because it still smells like candy. And it is purple."

Over time, you will come to have a handful of ways to recall prior learning. For example, you might bring out a chart from the day before, reading off each item while students point to places where they did that item. You might ask students to list "across their fingers" three things they learned about the topic at hand. This is a variation on those, for although it looks very different, the point again is to invite kids to consolidate what they have already learned, especially the aspects that are relevant to today's extension lesson.

❖ **Name the teaching point.**

"Today I want to teach you that when you have an opinion, when you judge something, you need to give *a couple of reasons*, not just one, and say details about each reason. If you write, 'For example . . .' or 'I think that because . . . ,' then that helps you bring in some details."

This minilesson is about elaboration, which is a quality of good writing across every genre. In stories, writers elaborate with dialogue and details about the setting and internal thoughts. In opinion writing, writers elaborate by telling more reasons and by supporting the reasons with information, examples, or description.

TEACHING

Retell an argument with no reasons, and contrast it with an argument with reasons. Let children know that strong arguments have reasons.

"Has it ever happened that you and someone in your family have different opinions about where you want to eat or what you want to do on a special day? Maybe one of you wants to go out for pizza, and someone else, for tacos. So you could just go like this:

'Pizza.'

'Tacos.'

'*Pizza*!'

'*Tacos*!'

'Pizza is *the* best!'

'No, tacos are *better*!'

"Do you think getting louder and louder is the best way to win the argument?" The children all chimed that no, that was no way to win an argument. I nodded. "You are so right! The better way to convince people is to give reasons that support your opinion. So you might say, 'I think we should go for pizza. *I think this because*, one, there is a nice place to sit at the pizza shop and so we can talk and have fun, *and*, two, pizza is better because it is cold out, and pizza will warm us up.'

"So, writers, when you want to convince your readers, it is important to write your opinion and to give lots of reasons. Think to yourself, 'After I tell my opinion, I'll give one reason and then talk a lot about it, and then I will give another reason, and talk a lot about it . . .'" I started the "Convince Your Reader!" anchor chart by placing two Post-its on chart paper.

"Here is a tip: when you want to say more about a reason for your opinion, it helps to say, 'I think this because . . .' or 'For example . . .'" I added a third Post-it to the chart.

Once again, this is a negative example of what not to do, so remember that you are just trying to make a quick point. Play this up; allow children to recognize themselves in this little argument and to laugh at themselves.

Make sure you play this up when you teach the minilesson. Keep the kids laughing and engaged.

When you list reasons for pizza, remember to use the graphic organizer of your fingers!

ACTIVE ENGAGEMENT

Divide children into groups. Ask each group to come up with and say more about their reasons for judging something as best.

"If you want to convince people of your opinion about the best item in your collection, it's usually important to say a few reasons and details about each reason. Instead of just saying, "The cocker spaniel is the best dog," it helps to give reasons why.

"Let's divide our class into quarters and then each quarter of the class can practice saying a couple of reasons for a judgment. We can use my dogs." I drew an imaginary line down the midpoint of the room starting from the front, going to the back, and starting from one side, going to the other. I showed the children in each quarter that they could pull together into a quick small group, then went from one group to another, giving each one dog from my pile, asking them to pretend for now that the dog I gave them was the group's candidate for "Best in Show."

"Talk together as a group, and gather some reasons why your dog is the best. As you come up with reasons, try to say more about your reasons, using 'I think this because . . .' and 'For example . . . .'" I pointed to the sentence starters.

Pretend to be a TV reporter, and interview a representative from one of the groups to learn what that group has selected as "Best in Show" and why.

After a few minutes, I said, "I'm from NBC, morning news, and I understand you were one of the judges for this dog show." The stunned "judge" giggled and nodded. "So can you tell all our viewers why you selected this collie as the 'Best in Show,' as your best dog?"

Miguel looked out over his audience. I whispered loud enough for all to hear, "Tell your reasons, Judge. Tell the audience why this dog is the one you think is the best."

Miguel nodded and ducked his head down to speak into my imaginary microphone, "The reason I chose the collie as the best dog is because the collie is the biggest."

I made an "add-on" gesture and whispered to Miguel, "Say more. 'I think this because . . .'"

Miguel said, "I think this is because big dogs are cool. She is bigger than my hand! And the other dogs are only up to my here," and he pointed to the knuckle of his thumb.

If children seem to need more scaffolding to do this well, you might invite the whole class to help the first judge say more, or you might tap other "judges."

"What do other judges think?" Soon Monique had announced that her small group had selected the cocker spaniel as the best. As I passed the microphone, I said in a stage whisper to the others, "Let's see if she gives several reasons,

Notice that in this instance, instead of suggesting children turn and talk to their partners, I've channeled them to work in four small groups. Children will appreciate the ways in which you vary the ways your teaching unfolds. But, of course, if it feels unnecessarily complex to orchestrate these groups, you can decide to continue relying on partnerships.

Once children are older, it will be common for you to suggest they stop and jot, but for now, jotting is time-consuming enough that you are much more apt to rely on children writing in the air. Teach them to actually dictate the words they will write rather than chatting about what they might write later.

Recruit a second judge only. You certainly won't call on half a dozen.

not just one. And let's see if she can say more about her reasons." Then I said, "So can you tell all our viewers why you selected the cocker spaniel as the best dog?"

"She's got the curliest hair."

Tapping the sentence starters on chart paper, I whispered to Monique, "Try, 'I think this because . . .'"

Monique popped out with "I think this because her fur is so curly I want to pat her!"

I repeated Monique's words and then turned to the class. "Turn to your neighbor, and help Monique say even more. Can you think of another reason why the cocker spaniel might be the best dog? Turn and talk."

LINK

Ask children to think back on what they've learned about writing in not only in the past few days but also in the past few months, and decide what to do to improve their writing and thinking today.

"So, writers, before you get started on today's work, let's take a moment to plan. Think about your own choices from your own collection, and think about the writing you did yesterday. Now, with all that you've learned about writing in the last few days, and since you started school," I gestured to the charts about writing around the room, "will you think of some ways in which you could improve on the writing you did yesterday?" I modeled thinking silently about writing plans for a moment, letting the children think for themselves.

"How many of you have plans to add onto what you wrote yesterday, thumbs up? Might some of you want to revise what you wrote—adding more reasons and more details and things like that? I've left some half-sheets of paper on your table, and some tape, revision strips, and some more pages that can be stapled together into books on your desks. Here is the biggest question of all: might there be a writer or two in this room who decide to do the *really* brave and hard-working choice—starting writing over, writing Draft Two? Because, of course, I have blank books and new award pages on your tables as well. So get started—and I will be admiring what you do."

I would have preferred for Monique to start at the beginning, saying, "I think my cocker spaniel is the best of all the dogs because she has the softest fur and the curliest."

Instead of moving in to hear more children's choices, recruit the class to extend what the one child has done.

Describe revision as brave work. It is!

Supporting Students in Elaboration

YOUR CONFERRING AND SMALL-GROUP WORK will be fast paced, complimentary, and responsive. You'll make sure you touch base with the majority of your writers, circulating to make sure that they are churning out writing at a nice clip. If you aren't entirely smitten with the work your students are producing, now is not a good time to show that, because your engagement with and support for their work is going to nourish their own engagement. So if a child has awarded a blue ribbon to a hair band and has just a tiny list of supportive reasons for that, the best response will be to look with great seriousness at her collection, to be spellbound with interest over the reasons for her evaluation—and to trust that your attentiveness will lead the writer to become more invested in this work.

If you worry that some of your writers have produced a page of work and now have that "I wrote a page and now I'm done" feeling, perhaps you might convene a small group that aims to teach writers to write more. You may decide to pull a group of writers and remind them that it is helpful to reread their writing, drawing on a toolkit of revision materials such as strips of paper, tape, and colored pens. The revision tools lure writers to produce reasons and examples. The chart you made during the minilesson—teaching children how to elaborate by saying "For example" and "I think that because"—can play a part in many of your conferences today. Of course, you'll also want to grant wait time for children, so resist the urge to jump in and offer examples of how to say more; instead touch one of the elaboration prompts, nod to the writer, and

MID-WORKSHOP TEACHING   Detailed Observations Are More Persuasive Than Sweeping Generalities

"Writers, can I have everyone's attention for a minute? Your pages are filling up with more and more reasons why you think one hair band or action figure is the best. And I appreciate that you are adding specific, detailed observations. In a minute, I want you to listen to the way that Katerina describes her best troll. She doesn't just go:

I love my troll. She is great. She is the GREATEST. I love LOVE LOVE!!! her. She is great, great, great.

"No way! Instead, Katerina adds specific details that come from really studying her favorite troll and noticing the tiniest details that make it special. Katerina, show the class your troll so they can think of their own details they might add to a piece about her."

Katerina circled the class, troll in hand. "People, think of exact words you could use to describe why you like the troll," I coached.

After the children talked for a minute, I said, "Class, listen as Katerina reads her writing, and let's give a thumbs up whenever she tells specific detailed observations about her troll."

Katerina read this, while I led the class in noting the detailed observations:

My best troll is the one with purple hair. I call her Wild Girl. Wild Girl is the best troll because she still has all her hair, except for one little bare spot. She is also the best because she has an outfit. It is a pink vest and some pink pants but her belly button still shows. I don't care about the belly button. I have other clothes for her from a old bear I got for Christmas but those clothes do not sparkle. They are the not-fancy clothes. Wild Girl's fancy clothes are very fancy and they do sparkle.

(continues)

"Writers, did you notice the way Katerina added very specific details to her writing? She talked about the one little bare spot in her troll's hair and how her shirt is so short that her belly button shows. It is clear that Katerina has studied her troll very, very closely, making very specific observations about it.

"Right now, take a moment to reread your writing. Are there places where you could write the way Katerina did, with very specific details? You can use a revision flap to make some changes."

As Students Continue Working . . .

"Writers, as you work, I want to remind you that a judge gives a red ribbon for second place, and a yellow ribbon for third place. Some of you are making whole books with pages for blue, red, yellow, and so on. Just be sure that you use your observing skills to write precise details supporting your opinions."

FIG. 2–1   Katerina includes specific details based on careful observations to support her opinion.

give a lean, yet firm, "Think about it, try it." Then, wait to see what the writer comes up with on her own. Be ready to respond to ideas, regardless of grandeur. Perhaps the child will respond simply, "I think it's best because it's pretty." Repeat the phrase, cradling each word as though it were gold, then tap the writer's paper to convey the urgency of getting those precious words down on the page. If Annabelle has written, "The strawberry sticker is the best sticker in my whole collection. When you scratch it, it smells like a bowl of strawberries!" then you can teach her, as well as the other writers in the group, to reread her writing and to elaborate by giving an example of one time when she tried scratching her sticker. It's not too much to hope that her writing will soon read, "The strawberry sticker is the best sticker in my whole collection. When I scratch it, it smells like a bowl of strawberries! One time I scratched it, and I could smell the strawberries on my sticker and I could smell strawberries on my finger! It is so so smelly, like jam."

You may also decide to gather a small group of writers who are stuck, who have produced a sentence stating their favorite item, and that is it. You'll want to try to figure out what is in their way. Presumably if they like a baseball card or a book best, they will have some reasons, so what is keeping them from writing those reasons? What you will probably find is that these youngsters are not, in fact, following the steps you laid out for judging fairly. They are probably not even going through the judging process at all. They just have a pile of cars, know that one is their favorite, and award that car their blue ribbon. When nudged to defend the choice, they generate one descriptor. "My blue car is the best because . . . it's cool."

You will want to remind this group of the process of judging. First the judge chooses a trait—say, color—and then considers the colors on each car and ranks the cars by color, with reasons one is the best in the Colors of My Cars contest. Then the judge considers the speed of the car, pushing each one off in a similar fashion and observing which rolls along the fastest. This, again, produces a car that outdoes the others. The winning car wins in several categories and these become reasons.

A Partner Talk Fishbowl

Channel writers to sit around the edges of the rug, and convene a partnership inside that frame, creating a "fishbowl" so that kids learn from watching others and from your voiceovers.

When the writers walked back to share today, I asked everyone to find their partner and move to the edge of the carpet and make a "fishbowl." There was some smiling from student to student as I told Boone and Tucker to move into the middle of the bowl to be our fish for the day. "Boone and Tucker are going to let us spy on their partner talk. They are going to show us how they talked about their writing, and we are going to listen to the things they say."

I gestured for Boone to begin. He said, "I wrote more writing today than I did yesterday. I made a blue ribbon piece and a red ribbon piece! I'm writing a lot. I only wrote one yesterday, and today two!" Boone touched the place in his piece where he had written more than the day before.

"Did you hear how Boone told *what he did* as a writer? He did not just read his writing to his partner and then say, 'I'm done.' He talked about what he did and tried to do when he was working." I added, "Your turn, Tucker!"

Tucker held up his writing and said, "See," showing off the length of it. Then he was silent. I said to the class, "Think about what hint you hope Boone whispers to Tucker. We don't just want him to show his final piece, we also want him to . . . what?"

Then Boone said, "You gotta say what you did, Tucker, like what you were trying to do."

Tucker slapped his hand over his mouth as if to say, "Oh, my gosh!" and then he said, "I put a lot of reasons in. I wrote a whole bunch, and I added little details and arrows to 'em."

I voiced over, "Tucker, I love the way you told your partner *what you did* as a writer today." Then I turned to the class and said, "Now you try. Partner 1, please go first."

"How Do I Write This Kind of Writing Well?"

IN THIS SESSION, you'll teach students that writers read and study the work of other writers and then try to incorporate what they have learned into their own writing.

GETTING READY

✔ Opinion Writing Checklist, Grades 1 and 2, copied onto chart paper, as well as individual copies for each student (see Connection, Teaching, and Active Engagement)

✔ Student writing folders and revision pens

✔ A white board and marker, or chart paper and marker, to record the kinds of writing students recall having written (see Connection)

✔ Enlarged copy of Brandon's writing as well as individual copies for students and Post-it notes (see Teaching and Active Engagement)

✔ Your own writing sample to be used to demonstrate spelling tricky words (see Mid-Workshop Teaching)

✔ "Ways to Spell Words" chart from the *Nonfiction Chapter Books* unit (see Mid-Workshop Teaching)

✔ Student writing folders, Post-it notes, pens (see Share)

COMMON CORE STATE STANDARDS: W.1.1, W.1.5, W.2.1, RI.1.1, RI.1.8, RL.1.1, RFS.1.2, RFS.1.3, SL.1.1, SL.1.2, L.1.1, L.1.2

THIS LESSON ASKS YOUNGSTERS to do a lot of challenging work. They are expected to recall the characteristics of good writing, and then to examine a text that represents a new kind of writing. They will be asked to make a comparison. How is the new kind of writing similar to texts they have admired before now—and how is it different? Finally, children will set goals for ways in which they can engage in substantial revisions of the writing they already made. This will help them to self-assess, applying criteria to their judgments of their own writing.

How often have you been asked to engage in such heady intellectual work? Think of the times a professor has asked you to collect and organize all you know about many different kinds of writing, to study an exemplar of a new kind of writing so as to identify the defining features of that writing, and to chart a course for yourself as you set out to make that kind of writing. Chances are fairly good that you haven't often been invited to participate in such heady intellectual work—and I suspect that reading this, you feel as I do. It would be fun.

Of course, it is not clear that six-year-olds will do a perfect job at any of this—nor would you or I. But learning can start with people giving something a go, plunging in to try their hand at the unknown. In fact, it's reasonable to suggest that once a learner has had a chance to try something, that learner is especially well positioned to learn.

In any case, today's teaching is an experiment. There is no question that you are inviting learners to participate in work where the cognitive demand is high. If your school studies Webb's Depths of Knowledge, then bring your colleagues and your principal in to see this lesson because this will be a time when you provide your students with a Level 4 lesson. And the important thing is for you to watch what happens to your children when you pose challenges like this for them.

The worst thing that can happen is that some of your children will show you they need more practice doing the high-level cognitive work of evaluating, monitoring their own learning, setting goals, and the like. The best thing that could happen is that your learners might be on fire, full of gritty resolve and high aspirations for the journey they'll make across this unit.

"How Do I Write This Kind of Writing Well?"

CONNECTION

Ask writers to list the kinds of writing they've learned to do this year and to list qualities of good writing for each of those kinds of writing. Set them up to create a similar list of qualities of strong opinion writing.

Before calling students to the meeting area, I placed a copy of the Opinion Writing Checklist on each child's rug spot, along with copies of the mentor text that we would be studying. "Writers, when you join me in the meeting area today, please bring your writing folder and your green revision pen. There are several things waiting for you on your rug spot. We won't need any of it for a little bit, so just put your folder on top of the pile and take a seat. Sound good?" Once all the students had joined me on the rug, I began.

"Writers, will you think back across this whole year of writing, and will you and your partner list across your fingers all the different kinds of writing you have learned to do?" Soon the room was filled with children listing what they'd learned. I gathered their attention and told them what I'd heard:

Kinds of Writing

◆ Small Moment stories

◆ How to (If/Then Curric)

◆ information (teaching books) writing

"If we thought about each of these kinds of writing, would we be able to say ways writers do that kind of writing well? Let's try it. I'll call out one kind of writing, and you and your partner see if you can, quick as a wink, list ways to do that kind of writing well." I waited, looked around as if I was collecting racers on the starting line, and then said, "Small Moments: what do you do to write Small Moments well? List across your fingers."

After a minute, I said, "You guys are good. You ready for something harder?" I again waited, as if letting the racers come to the starting line. "Think just about teaching books (also called information writing, or all-about writing). List across your fingers ways to do that kind of writing well!"

Someone once said that a fiction writer's hardest task is moving a character from here to there. Moving a whole class of kids is no easy feat either! It's like moving a school of minnows.

Throughout these units of study, you'll find that we encourage you to let kids in on the larger principles that inform your teaching. Just as I want you to understand the logic of these units so that you can create your own, you want children to understand the logic of your work with any particular kind of writing, because you want children to grow up learning not just the specifics that you teach about particular kinds of writing, but learning, also, how to go about studying and producing any kind of writing. In this portion of the lesson, you let the kids in on the logic that informs some of your teaching, and you connect today's teaching not just to yesterday's, as is commonplace, but also to your yearlong curriculum.

"You know a lot about all those kinds of writing," as I gestured to our list. "But now, writers, we are working on a kind of writing that you haven't done yet this year. The job that a writer has when starting a new kind of writing is to look closely at the work other people have done and think, 'How do writers make this kind of writing really good? What did that writer do that I could try, too?'

"Writers, the writing you are working on in this unit is writing about ideas, about thoughts. That is especially challenging because instead of writing about what you do and what you know—the facts—you are writing your ideas, your thoughts. People actually call this kind of writing 'opinion writing' because the writer tells his or her opinion, his or her ideas."

❖ **Name the teaching point.**

"Today I want to teach you that when you write something, it is important to understand the kind of writing you are doing and to figure out ways people do that kind of writing really well. Then, you can try to do those things in your own writing."

Always notice that throughout these books we glorify work that is harder and assume that for any writer, the invitation to tackle something that is challenging will be an appealing one. When teaching writing, one can also teach values in general, and Carol Dweck's research reminds us all that children profit from growing up in a culture that values hard work.

TEACHING AND ACTIVE ENGAGEMENT

Set up children to study a piece of writing, comparing it to the Opinion Writing Checklist to find and name attributes of effective opinion writing.

"So, this is the challenge: how do people write *opinion* writing really well? One way to answer that big question is to look closely at some really good opinion writing and find out what that writer did.

"Just like those dog show judges use a checklist to help them figure out which dog is the 'Best in Show,' writers use checklists, too." I pointed to the Opinion Writing Checklist for Grades 1 and 2, and gestured toward the small copies on the rug in front of them.

"This is the checklist that you'll use this year, in first grade, to set goals and reflect on the progress you are making as opinion writers. Remember, this is old news! You've seen charts like this before, when you thought about narrative writing and about information writing. The only thing that makes this chart different is that it is about opinion writing.

Opinion Writing Checklist

	Grade 1	NOT YET	STARTING TO	YES!	Grade 2	NOT YET	STARTING TO	YES!
	Structure				**Structure**			
Overall	I wrote my opinion or my likes and dislikes and said why.	☐	☐	☐	I wrote my opinion or my likes and dislikes and gave reasons for my opinion.	☐	☐	☐
Lead	I wrote a beginning in which I got readers' attention. I named the topic or text I was writing about and gave my opinion.	☐	☐	☐	I wrote a beginning in which I not only gave my opinion, but also set readers up to expect that my writing would try to convince them of it.	☐	☐	☐
Transitions	I said more about my opinion and used words such as *and* and *because*.	☐	☐	☐	I connected parts of my piece using words such as *also, another*, and *because*.	☐	☐	☐
Ending	I wrote an ending for my piece.	☐	☐	☐	I wrote an ending in which I reminded readers of my opinion.	☐	☐	☐
Organization	I wrote a part where I got readers' attention and a part where I said more.	☐	☐	☐	My piece had different parts; I wrote a lot of lines for each part.	☐	☐	☐
	Development				**Development**			
Elaboration	I wrote at least one reason for my opinion.	☐	☐	☐	I wrote at least two reasons and wrote at least a few sentences about each one.	☐	☐	☐
Craft	I used labels and words to give details.	☐	☐	☐	I chose words that would make readers agree with my opinion.	☐	☐	☐
	Language Conventions				**Language Conventions**			
Spelling	I used all I knew about words and chunks of words (*at, op, it*, etc.) to help me spell.	☐	☐	☐	To spell a word, I used what I knew about spelling patterns (*tion, er, ly*, etc.).	☐	☐	☐
	I spelled all the word wall words right and used the word wall to help me spell other words.	☐	☐	☐	I spelled all of the word wall words correctly and used the word wall to help me figure out how to spell other words.	☐	☐	☐

"I'm going to take a moment and read over the items on this checklist, and you can follow along on your own copies. As I'm sure you can see, there are a *lot* of things that opinion writers need to do to make their writing strong and powerful. On this side, you'll notice what opinion writers in first grade are expected to do." I pointed to each item as I read through it on the checklist. Then, I moved toward the right column of the checklist. "There are also things on this checklist that second-grade opinion writers are expected to do. But maybe, *you* are doing some of these things already! You are growing so fast and learning so much!"

The Opinion Writing Checklist, Grades 1 and 2, can be found on the CD-ROM.

"So now that we have an idea of what makes opinion writing strong and powerful, let's look at Brandon's writing and see how he measures up. Brandon is a boy your age, and you each have a copy of his writing right in front of you. (See Figure 3–1.) Let's read it together, and then we'll come back to this checklist and see what he did." I displayed an enlarged copy of Brandon's writing and then read it aloud.

> All the bugs in my collection are gross and that is cool! I like a lot of the bugs but the one I like best is the Giant Pinching beetle because its pinchers really grip things, even someone's finger. When you squeeze its back, the pinchers snap close. The beetle is better than the fly even though the fly's eyes are cool and glossy green. The beetle is better because it's bigger and because the fly doesn't do anything good like pinch things, it just stays still. Today I made the beetle grab the fly and pinch it and then I pretended it ate the fly for its dinner.

"Now let's look at some of those bullet points and see how Brandon's writing compares." I thought aloud as I ticked through some of the bullet points, modeling for the students how I compared a mentor text to established criteria. "Okay, '*I wrote my opinion or my likes and dislikes and said why.*' Brandon certainly did write his opinion. I know that he likes the bugs in his collection, and that the giant pinching beetle is his favorite. He says it right there." I pointed out that line in Brandon's writing. "Okay, what else? '*I wrote at least one reason for my opinion.*' Hmm . . . it looks like one of the reasons why the beetle is his favorite is because the pinchers really grip things. Look, he said that the pinchers can even grab someone's fingers! So that's one reason."

Pass the baton to children, pulling back to let them carry on where you left off. Then convene the class.

"Writers, now it's your turn. Take a few minutes with your partner, and check how Brandon's writing measures up to some of the other bullet points. Did he write an ending for his piece? Did he make his writing easy to read?" I gave the class a few minutes to turn and talk, listening in on their conversations so I could help focus the group when we came back together.

"So, what did you think? How did Brandon's writing measure up to the Opinion Writing Checklist?"

"He did better than he was supposed to!" shouted Miguel.

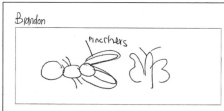

FIG. 3–1   Brandon's collection writing provides students with an exemplar, serving as a visual support for the expectations outlined by the checklist.

"What do you mean by that?" I asked.

"Well, he was supposed to give at least one reason that he liked his beetle the best, but I count three reasons!" said Miguel. "He must really love his bugs, I'd love to see them, too!"

"He put a lot of periods. Every time the sentence is over, he used punctuation. And over there, he put an exclamation point," Katerina remarked.

"You are absolutely right, Katerina! Ending each sentence with a punctuation mark helps make Brandon's writing so much easier for us to read," I reinforced.

LINK

Ask writers to compare their writing to the Opinion Writing Checklist and then make a plan for today's writing.

"Okay, writers, before you go off to write today, I'd like you to take a moment and compare your own writing to the Opinion Writing Checklist. I'll read through the highlighted items on our checklist again, and this time, use your revision pen to find places in your writing where you are *already* doing those things. Then you can draw a star right there in your writing! Do you remember what you do if you can't find a place in your writing where you are doing something from the checklist?"

"Shoot for the stars!" kids exclaimed with arms shooting toward the ceiling.

"That's right. Draw a star beside the things on the checklist that you need to work on next! Okay then, let's get started!" I read through each bullet on the checklist, giving students a chance to look over their opinion writing, evaluating their work and making plans for revision. Once students had finished evaluating their writing, I asked them to make plans for the day's writing. "How many of you think you might reread all the opinion writing you have been doing and think about ways you can make that writing better, shooting for the stars?" Many so indicated.

After a bit, I said, "Once you know what you will be doing today, get yourself started. You can leave the meeting area when you have a plan ready for what you will be doing today. If you need some extra help, stay right here on the rug."

Notice that, as always, only a few children actually talk into the whole group. This is deliberate because we're always working to save time for writing. Any portion of a minilesson could easily become long-winded if you don't guard time.

You'll become accustomed to reading about ways we support youngsters to use these checklists. This time, we provide less support than we did earlier. We don't read each item aloud and leave time for children to assess their work in relation to that item. The fact that children now work with more independence shouldn't surprise you.

Conferring to Help Students Draw on Learning from Prior Units of Study

ALWAYS, AT THE START OF A NEW UNIT, one of the most efficient things you can do is to remind writers to continue to draw on all they learned in previous units. You may, for example, want to bring out charts from earlier units that especially pertain to children's work today, making those charts front and center in your children's writing.

This, too, may be the day that you lead small-group work to convey to the students who never go back to rework completed writing that they need to draw a line in the sand, decide "that was then and this is now." Writers revise. It will be important for writers to know that they should be able to initiate revision without needing you at

---

MID-WORKSHOP TEACHING   **Sk-ska-skating to Hear and Spell All the Chunks in a Word**

"Writers? Pens down, eyes up," I said, stepping toward the "Ways to Spell Words" chart. "I want to teach you another way to make sure your spelling is its very best, especially on the trickiest of tricky words. Many of you use this same strategy as a reader, so let me teach you how to say and listen to each part of the word by *sk-ska-skating* across the word and writing the parts you hear."

I enlarged a piece of my own writing and modeled how to *sk-ska-skate* across a word to do my best spelling. I said, "I want to spell the word *undercoat*, but it is a tricky word. Watch how I sk-ska-skate across it. First I say the entire word slow and stretchy, 'u-n-d-e-r-c-o-a-t.' Now I say each part of the word I hear, and I sk-ska-skate across each part and write it on my page." I said the first part of the word, "un," and wrote it. Then I said the next part I heard, "der," and I added a "der" so the word now read "under." Then I said the last part of the word, "coat," and I added that to the other two parts so the word read, "undercoat."

"There," I said, "I sk-ska-skated across the word, listening and writing each part I heard. I'm not sure it is perfect, so I will put a circle around it to remind myself to go back during editing, but it is as close as I can get right now."

"I have a great idea! Right now, just like at the roller rink, let's have an *all-skate* dance. Everybody, as you keep writing, when you get to a tricky word, try to

sk-ska-skate across the word! I'll put some music on while you do your best skating. Each time you find a word that you need to sk-ska-skate across, after you skate across it, stand up and do a little skate around your desk to show the other writers how you are skating through the tricky-to-spell words!"

As the students began spelling and skating, I added the new spelling strategy to our spelling chart so that it now read:

> ### Ways to Spell Words
>
> - Say it, slide it, hear it, write it.
> - Use snap words.
> - Listen for little words inside.
> - Sk-ska-skate across the word.

---

their side. Part of this is making sure that there are accessible revision tools readily available at every table.

One way to be prepared to teach students to reread and revise completed writing is for you to carry your own writing folder with you as you confer, making sure that your folder contains a bunch of opinion writing. That way, you can model how you go back to every piece and add more onto each. You'll say, "It's not enough to only make *one* of my pieces as good as I can. No way! Now that I know how to do all of these amazing writing moves, I must, must, must revise all the way through my folder! That's how I make my writing muscles bigger and bigger!"

I sat beside Roselyn as she opened up to her piece about her favorite Tech Deck skateboard toy. I asked Roselyn if I could take a peek at her writing folder while she worked. She nodded and began to reread her current piece. Although it can be hard, I try to resist the urge to act solely off of the current piece of writing with which students are engaged. Instead I take a moment to assess pieces across the folder, looking for patterns that writers display across several pieces of writing. These patterns often depict areas of greatest need. I find that by doing this I have much more important data to inform the best way in which I should proceed with each conference.

As I looked across the two pieces in Roselyn's folder and read the current piece over her shoulder, it became clear to me that while Roselyn included several reasons in her writing, along with some examples, she would benefit from strategies to help her elaborate further on her opinions.

I complimented Roselyn, saying "Roselyn, you do something in all of your opinion writing that makes it very convincing. You don't just include *one* reason why you like something, you include *lots* of reasons, and you even give examples to go with those reasons." I pointed out several places across her writing where she had done this.

Beaming, Roselyn said, "You have to put details in your writing to make it good, like here, I put the colors it comes in," she pointed to her page.

"You are right. That detail helps your writing. And Roselyn, one tip I have is that when you do something that really works in a piece of writing, it usually helps to do that thing a lot, not just once. Are there other places where you could use your talent for adding details and add still more details?"

As she reread, she realized another detail she wanted to tag on, and soon she'd pulled a revision strip from the basket at the middle of the table and scrawled out an additional sentence (see Figure 3–3).

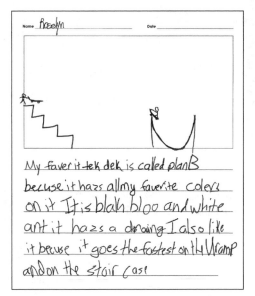

My favorite Tech Deck is called Plan B because it has all my favorite colors on it. It is black, blue and white and it has a drawing. I also like it because it goes the fastest on the U Ramp and on the staircase.

FIG. 3–2   Roselyn's collection draft includes several reasons using detailed observations, but has opportunities for elaboration.

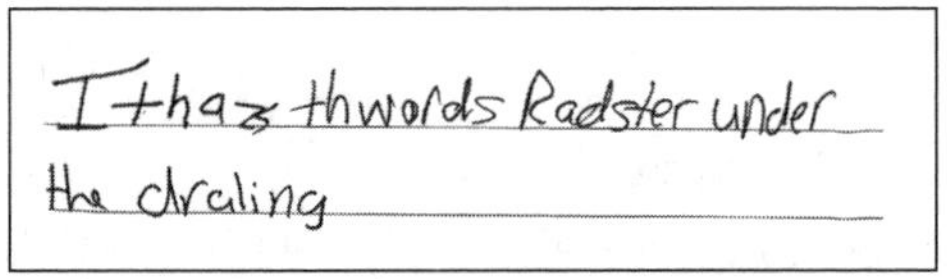

It has the words "Radster" under the drawing.

FIG. 3–3   Roselyn used a spiderleg to add more.

I pointed out to Roselyn that she might add more details later, after I moved on to another child, and then she could check that item off on her checklist. "And then, then you could see what else the checklist says that you could try," I said, expecting that to be a closing for the conference.

Roselyn, however, immediately scanned the checklist, and said, "Oh! I can tell a little story. Like when I played with my Tech Deck at home, and it was so cool because it kept flipping over and over!"

"Now all you need to do is to decide where in your writing that might fit best," I said. "It helps to reread your piece from the beginning and think, 'Where can I add this?'"

Before concluding the conference, I restated the work Roselyn had done in a way that would make it transferable across all her writing, as well as urged her to continue this with each and every piece in her folder. "So, Roselyn, remember whenever you are working on a piece of writing, it is important to think about *everything* you have learned. You can use the charts in the classroom to help you, too. I bet you can find places to make the other writing in your folder just as amazing as this piece! After all, you're so much smarter already about this kind of writing. You can make the pieces you wrote earlier this week even better using all you know now!"

Later, after the workshop was over, I noticed Roselyn had added this flap onto her draft:

> One time I Put it on a box at home
> The box was About 10 inches long and
> i used my fingrs to fflip it over
> It fliped two times in the air and
> it landed on its weels It was soo
> cool I tryed to do it again but I
> culdnt do it

One time I put it on a box at home. The box was about 10 inches long and I used my fingers to flip it over. It flipped two times in the air and it landed on its wheels. It was so cool! I tried to do it again but I couldn't do it.

FIG. 3–4   Roselyn revised to include an anecdote that supports her opinion.

Writers Set Goals

Channel students to set goals for their writing by rereading and using anchor charts around the classroom.

Today's work was ambitious, and I knew, even before calling students back to the meeting area, that they would be hesitant about putting their writing away, insisting on more time to finish the big plans they had set off to do. I decided that now would be an important time to talk up the value of goals.

"Writers, I can see that you're hard at work! Bring your folders, as well as a Post-it note and your writing pen, to your spot in the meeting area. Don't worry if you're not finished because you'll be able to keep going with your writing tomorrow!" Once the students had gathered, I began, "Today, you looked at the Opinion Writing Checklist and then each of you made big plans for the work you wanted to get done today. But sometimes our plans are *so* big that it's hard to imagine getting it all done! Do *you* sometimes feel as if you don't have enough time to finish everything?"

Many faces nodded back at me in agreement. "Well, here's a top-secret tip." I peered over each shoulder, then leaned in close to whisper intently, "You can set your own goals!" The children stared back with wide-open eyes. "Professional athletes set goals all the time—how many home runs they'll hit, or points they'll score, or how many new tricks they'll learn. Writers can do that, too! You can think, 'How long am I going to work on this piece, and what am I going to do next?' or 'How many sentences will I write? How many more pages will I add?' You can set a goal and stick to it by recording your goal so you remind yourself what *big* plans you have for writing workshop each day.

"Think about the goals you'd like to set for yourself. Look back at the pieces in your folder, and let's spend the next few minutes making plans for tomorrow. Be sure to jot down a few words to remind yourself of your goals."

I voiced over as students recorded their plans, "You can even make different notes for different goals and put them on the pieces in your folder! Maybe you'll use the charts in the room to think about strategies you want to push yourself to try. Maybe you'll count your sentences, or how many pages you have already, to set a goal to write longer." As children worked, I coached in to help writers set strong and attainable goals.

I reconvened the group to prompt them to carry this goal-setting work into the coming days and weeks. "Keep these Post-it notes right in your folder because you'll use them to get started on your writing tomorrow. When you reach your goal, or even pass your goal, you can pick up your note, read it out loud, then crumple it up, and kiss it goodbye! That way, you can make more notes to set new, bigger, and bolder goals each and every time you write!"

Making an analogy helps engage young writers in the work of goal-setting, while encouraging children to reflect on their writing to make purposeful plans for their pieces.

Opinion Writers Expect Disagreement

THIS SESSION BEGINS with you weighing the pluses and minuses of various book covers and proposing a rather outlandish choice for the best one, knowing that children will definitely disagree with your opinion. "How many of you agree that this book cover is the best?" you ask, knowing full well that most won't agree. Think back to all the minilessons when you have said, "Is this the way to be a good partner?" and then acted in a way that you knew would produce cries of "No way!" Or other times, when you said, "Is this what writers do when they finish their writing?" and then you wrote a last line and flicked the writing out of view, never to be reconsidered again. Often, you extol the characteristics of good work by contrasting the ideal with not-so-good work.

Today, you use this method to help draw attention to a new characteristic of effective opinion writing. The *method* you use is that of contrasting what's good with what's less good—and interestingly enough, the characteristic of effective opinion writing that you are spotlighting is that when judging something as good, you can highlight your judgment by pointing out what would not be good. That is, you essentially let kids in on the fact that opinion writing gets its life force from the fact that the writer is not just saying one item or one idea is good, that writer is also saying the one item or idea is better than others, that it can be contrasted with other options that are less good.

This lesson goes one step farther. It begins to introduce a concept that children will be learning for many years, and that is the fact that the real challenge in opinion writing—and the life force in this genre—comes from the fact that people do not all agree. Why bother to provide reasons and examples and evidence in support of an opinion save for the fact that others see things differently? That is, this lesson introduces counterargument.

It is interesting to note that despite the Common Core State Standards' tremendous focus on opinion and argument writing, the standards do not pay any heed to the place of a counterargument until writers are in sixth grade. Our opinion is that postponing the existence of a contrary opinion until sixth grade is too late. We believe that opinions get their life force through counterarguments. This lesson, in a very child-centered way, illuminates that.

IN THIS SESSION, you'll teach students that writers don't always share the same opinion. When people disagree, this leads writers to back up their opinions with reasons.

GETTING READY

✔ The dullest, most boring book cover you can find to use as a model; we suggest taking the festive jacket off a well-loved book so that only the plain, woven cover remains (see Connection)

✔ Students' shoebox collections set out on the tables, with their "Best in Show" choices highlighted (see Teaching and Active Engagement)

✔ Chart paper, marker (see Link)

✔ Student writing folders (see Share)

✔ "Convince Your Reader!" chart (see Share)

COMMON CORE STATE STANDARDS: W.1.1, W.2.1, RFS.1.3.g, SL.1.1, SL.1.2, SL.1.3, L.1.1.g,j; L.1.2, L.1.6

Opinion Writers Expect Disagreement

CONNECTION

Announce that you like a particular book cover better than others, choosing one that you know the kids won't like, thereby setting up the students to have an opinion that counters yours.

"How many of you agree with me that, of all the book covers on this year's read-aloud books, this book cover is the best?" I purposely pointed to the least colorful, least likely-to-be-popular cover, differentiating it from a long row of more beautiful book covers, propped up along the chalk tray. "If you agree with me, stay perfectly silent. If you have a *different* opinion, turn and tell your partner *your* opinion."

I paused just for a second for the chatter to be heard. "Wow. I thought you would all agree with me—after all, I'm the grown-up. But you certainly have your own opinions. Let me just clarify. How many of you agreed that the book cover I like is fantastic?"

No one indicated that they agreed. I feigned astonishment. One child called out, "I like this one," and pointed to the cover of *Charlotte's Web*.

"How many of you liked the *Charlotte's Web* book cover the best?" More hands shot up, but many called out other choices. "We don't all agree, do we? We think different things. That's pretty exciting! Maybe, if we heard each other's reasons for liking one cover or another—or one dog or another, one hair band or another—we might change our own minds or grow our thinking, which, of course, is one of the best things in the world to do."

Explain that when putting opinions out into the world, writers expect some will hold contrary views.

"Writers, not only is it exciting that in one class of first-graders there are lots of different opinions about which book cover is best, it is also important. The only way that the other kids in this class (and in this whole school and this whole world) can know what you think, what your opinion is, is for you put your opinion out into the world. People may say, 'I agree with you.' People also may say, 'I disagree with you.'

"You will want to learn what people don't like about your opinion about your book cover or your choice of the best dog or hair band—because maybe they'll convince you or change your mind. Also, if you know what people think, you can talk back for your choice. You can be more persuasive."

In an earlier minilesson, you reenacted a family quarrel over what to eat: pizza or tacos, and children agreed that simply yelling one's opinion louder and louder is no way to get one's opinion across and convince others. This time, you again highlight what you want to say by using a contrasting example.

❖ Name the teaching point.

"Today I want to teach you that writers don't all agree and that's okay! If one person has written his or her opinion, someone else can say, 'I agree. My opinion is the same,' or, 'I disagree. I have a different opinion.' When we don't agree with someone else's opinion, that's a good time to write our own opinion and back it up with reasons *why* we disagree or think something different."

TEACHING AND ACTIVE ENGAGEMENT

Coach children to rehearse writing an opinion about a collection other than their own, using what they now know is required in effective opinion writing.

"I wonder—since people think differently—if you have ever looked at someone else's collection and thought, 'I think differently.' Have you ever looked at what someone else says is their best car or dog or baseball card or book and then thought, 'No way that I think that's the best!' Because if you have ever read or heard someone else's opinion and thought, 'I disagree,' that's a good time to . . . to do what?" Some kids called out that this was a time to write their own opinions, and I nodded. "You are right. When you hear or read an opinion and think, 'I have a different opinion,' that's a good time to write your own opinion.

"Are you ready to try something we have never ever done? In a minute, let's make one little part of our minilesson include a time for you to walk absolutely silently around the classroom, looking at the collections that your friends have laid out, noticing their 'Best in Show' choices. And will you think about whether maybe, just maybe, there is an instance when your friend has one opinion and you have another? If you find one of those places, give me a thumbs up, from wherever you are. You ready? Zip your mouths closed, and open your eyes so you can really, really look. Off you go! You have two minutes only."

After two minutes, I reconvened the class on the rug. "Did any of you look at someone else's opinion and think, 'I disagree'?" Children all signaled that yes, they'd had their own ideas. "This is such a class of strong thinkers, ready to make up your own minds!"

LINK

Send children off to writing time, inviting them to write counterarguments, and reminding them to rely on all they've learned about effective opinion writing.

"So, writers, today you are going to have a chance to write your opinions about *other people's* collections. This time, though, your writing is going to be extra powerful because there will end up being two opinions beside a collection, with one person saying, 'I think *this* is the best and here's why' and another saying, 'I disagree. I think, instead, that *this* is the best, and here's why.' Remember when we talked about your family arguments over where to eat—Tacos! Pizza! *Tacos!*—and we decided that the best way to convince people is to write your opinion, writing really well. You'll want to remember what we know about good opinion writing."

Imagine the classroom with collections of action figures, plastic horses, hair bands, and the like set up along the windowsill, the counter, the back table, with each collection containing some blue ribbon and red ribbon selections, showcased with pieces of writing that extol their virtues. Now . . . into that mix . . . comes counterarguments! What excitement!

Notice that I'm not suggesting children write contrasting opinions by listing the reasons they don't like their friend's item. That could hurt feelings.

"Right now—quietly—write your opinion of another person's collection 'in the air.' Now in your mind, say a reason for your opinion. Oh, I can see from the sparkles in your eyes, you have so much to say! It is going to be so interesting to hear all the different opinions developing about these collections. That is so much more interesting than when everyone just goes along and agrees, without really thinking and looking closely.

"So I'm not going to say, 'Get going to your writing spot,' because I guess what you will do today is to go to the places around the room where people have their collections set up, and their opinion writing, too. And you'll look over your friend's collection, decide which item *you* think is the best one, and then you'll see if your friend agreed or thought differently. So your writing will either start, 'I agree with . . . I think . . . is the best . . . in this collection.' Or you will start your writing by saying, 'I disagree with . . . I do not think . . . is the best in this collection. Instead, I think . . .' and you'll be off and writing!"

I had already put the words I was suggesting children use on large chart paper, and now I displayed them prominently. Save time, when you can, by doing this writing ahead of time.

Counterargument Requires Respectful Attention to Opposing Views and Complex Sentence Structure

IT IS HELPFUL FOR YOU TO APPROACH THE DAY'S WRITING WORKSHOP with a clear sense of a progression of work that you expect to see from more novice writers to more proficient writers. When teaching writers the skills of counterargument, one of the progressions you'll note relates to the treatment given to the opposing view. The more novice writer will either ignore other views altogether, simply presenting his or her opinion, or this writer will speak in black-and-white terms, defiantly disagreeing and dismissing everything that another person has said. The writer who is just starting to learn counterargument will sling around terms such as, "It is stupid to say that the collie is the best dog. It is *ugly*! It is *horrible*. You are all wrong, wrong, wrong." The far more sophisticated counterargument would go like this, "I can understand why you'd argue that the collie is the best dog. It is a very impressive dog, with soft fur, and a proud way of walking. Although the collie has some good features, I still think that the flat-coated retriever is an even more impressive dog. Like the collie, it. . . . In addition, it. . . ." This progression should make sense to you. After all, the thoughtful people in your own life are probably the people who are not inflexible in their thinking, nor do they dismiss every idea that is different than their own. Instead, they are willing to entertain ideas that are different than their own.

Now, I am in no way suggesting that first-graders will become skilled at entertaining each other's ideas and will be able to adjust their own opinions to show that they've taken into account counterarguments. But it is helpful for you to approach today's teaching confident that considering the other person's choice carefully and respectfully is not just what polite people do, this is also what a skilled debater does. And actually, perhaps the highest goal of all is for a person to listen to the counterargument and revise his or her original argument to take into account part of the counterargument. So absolutely, you will want to teach children some of the phrases they can use that can help them to show respectful attention to the ideas they will be disagreeing with.

(continues)

MID-WORKSHOP TEACHING
Use the Transition *Because* and Spell It Well

After students had been circulating for a while, I asked them to stop and listen. "Writers, I know you have been working to make sure others can read your opinions. Everyone is reading everything! Here's a tip: in every kind of writing there are particular words that writers end up needing to spell a lot. Opinion writers need the word *because*. You often want to tell people the reasons for your choices, and so you want to write, 'I think this because . . .' But *because* is not an easy word to spell, and stretching it out doesn't help you get any closer to spelling it right. It is a word that needs to be spelled in a snap and that is why it lives on our word wall! Eyes on the word wall. Find 'because.' It goes like this: 'B-E-C-A-U-S-E.'

"Right now, will you look at the spelling of *because* and notice interesting things about how it is spelled?" I gave the children a moment of silence to think about this. "Tell your partner what you notice," I said. Soon I'd called on a few children.

Bradley announced, "The *b* is tall and then it is all small."

Skylee added, "There are a whole pile of vowels. And you can't sound them out. They don't make any sense."

I agreed. "This is not a word that you'll want to stretch out and try to spell that way. It is easier to just chant it and get it into your mind. Can you all say it with me: b-e-c-a-u-s-e, because, because, because.

"Before you continue writing, will you reread what you have written so far with your partner? I am pretty sure you will find that you have used this word—*because*—in your writing. So fix up the spelling of it, okay? Try and spell it in a snap if you can, but if not, check and use the word wall to get it spelled just right."

Be prepared, in your conferring and small-group work, to leave behind cheat sheets such as this one:

Some Polite and Thoughtful Ways to Disagree with Another Person's Opinion

- Some people think . . . They say . . . This makes sense because . . . Still I think . . .
- I can understand why . . . thinks . . . but I disagree. I think that . . . is even more. . . . I think this because . . .
- In my opinion, . . . is the (best). . . . I know other . . . , but I still think . . . is the best.

One of the challenges in this work is that it requires not just more careful looking, more evidence, and, ideally, more discussion of the evidence, but it also requires more complex sentence structures. This is also an opportune time, then, to pull together a small group of your writers who need help using more sophisticated sentence structures. After all, this is the work expected of first-graders by the Common Core Language Standards. Bring together children who tend to write in a series of short thoughts, perhaps linked together with conjunctions such as *and* or *so*.

You might decide to devote a few minutes of your small-group time to playing a version of "Conjunction Junction." Make index cards with the words *but*, *also*, and *because*. Then show children that they can sometimes use words like these to join two of their sentences together. You might decide to use these words to link together the sentences in a simple piece you produce for the occasion.

This game is not about right and wrong but about exploring ways sentences can sound and look. *"I like the black lab the best. He has silky black hair"* can become *"I like the black lab the best* because *he has silky black hair."* You could reach for higher goals: *"Although I like the collie, I like the flat-coated retriever even better!"* (Guess what kind of dog *I* own?) Oral rehearsal and verbal play are surefire ways to develop more complex sentence construction.

Be sure to keep this work short, explicit, and, above all, fun so that children may return to their writing spots to compose new sentences, or revise old ones, energized with the growing understanding of ways to incorporate more complex sentence structure into their own writing.

Whenever you find yourself incorporating language and word-study instruction into writing workshop, be mindful of where your writers fall across the stages of language development and spelling acquisition. It is unwise to ask a new English language learner to construct, or worry, about compound sentence construction as a beginning writer. That work develops through oral language by listening, speaking, and having conversations with peers. Rely on the research and wise words of Marie Clay who taught us, "The longest utterance a child can make predicts what they can read and write. So when they burst into your classroom and they tell you a story, you can think about what they are saying and how they are saying it and how that matches with the books they read and what they are writing." Hold fast to this knowledge as you support students with language development.

Strategies for Persuasion

Pretend to be a new child in the room, and get the class reteaching you, a pretend novice, what they've learned about writing opinions well. Elicit the value of reasons, at a minimum.

"Writers, we talked about how the best way to get someone to go for pizza or to agree on your choice of the best dog or bracelet or Lego man is not just to *yell* your opinion louder and louder. So can you pretend I am a new kid to this class, and will some of you tell me how a person *does* convince people of their opinion?"

I jumped out of my seat at the front of the meeting area and walked into the room like I was a little lost child. "Hi, I'm new to the class," I said, trying to make my voice seem like I was a new six-year-old. "I heard I gotta write about my best thing—best color or whatever—and show people why it's my best. Can I just go like this"—and I tightened my face, my fists, my voice, and said with great intensity—"ORANGE! Is that how you show people your opinion?"

The kids all climbed up on their knees, trying to talk at once. "You gotta say *why*," they said. "You gotta tell 'because' and have reasons. Like why not red? Or purple?"

"Oh!" I said, as if all this was totally new to me. "So good opinion writers say their opinion and then say reasons. Like . . . ? What would my reasons be? I like orange because I do."

"Maybe it makes you happy 'cause it is not dull," one child volunteered. "Or because Halloween is your favorite holiday?" another one said.

"Oh! I got it." I tried again. "I like orange because it is a happy color, and I have a lot of orange clothes?"

"*And*, you gotta use nice words like sparkly diamonds," Will announced, and based on this, the class was soon helping me use sparkly words to pump up the value of the color orange.

Channel writers to show each other ways they have used to make their own writing convincing. Harvest what children say to give the class yet more options.

"So right now, will you show each other what *you* have done in your writing to be convincing? Turn and talk."

Awarding Booby Prizes for More Practice—and More Fun

ear Teachers,

The session we suggest here is entirely optional. It could be shrunk and turned into a mid-workshop teaching point on any day, it could be a teaching point that you postpone until the next bend in the road of this unit, or it could be a way to keep kids engaged in the basic work of this unit. We leave that choice up to you.

Whenever someone is learning a new skill, that learning requires repeated practice. Your kids are not only learning the skill of opinion writing—learning to provide reasons to support an opinion, to shift from generalization to detail, to organize their text, to generate and then record ideas—they are also learning to form letters, to spell, to punctuate, to use lower- and uppercase letters appropriately, to consider noun/verb agreement, and to include modifiers. So simply giving kids more time to write, and more purposes for writing—especially purposes that motivate them, as this one will—can be a good thing.

In this session, you remind students that judges sometimes give out booby prizes to the worst specimen of their own collection. To do this, they will need to go through the same judging moves as before. That is, if a child has five plastic action figures and decides that the one trait that matters is the amount of firepower that a superhero has in his possession, then the figure with only a slingshot may be ranked last. If the assessor determines that the amount of muscles matter, this factor may again weigh against the lad with just a slingshot. The assessor—the writer—can decide that of all the plastic figures in his collection, this one is his least impressive.

You'll see that we've tucked in some specific lessons that you can embed into this minilesson, and that we couldn't resist a share session that lets children in on the fact that many of the great stories in our world are stories about the underdog who ends up having surprising strengths. You may or may not decide to bring out those sensibilities.

The main point of the lesson is that it is fun, and it will motivate children to gain yet more practice determining traits upon which to judge, judging with careful attention to evidence (not leaping to rash opinions), and then writing evidence-based, descriptive,

COMMON CORE STATE STANDARDS: W.1.1, W.1.5, W.2.1, RI.1.8, SL.1.1, L.1.1, L.1.2

and, hopefully, objective defenses for their decisions. The more automatic these moves become, the more new learning about writing in general and opinion writing in particular children will be ready to take on. If you detect that these moves are already automatic for your children, that would be a good reason to skip this session entirely. If only some children need more work with these moves, the suggestions here could become small-group work or homework.

MINILESSON

One of the best ways to start a minilesson is by referencing the good work that your children have done. It's thrilling to kids to hear that you talk about them and think about them outside of school, so you might tell them about how, the evening before, you brought their work somewhere—to the coffee shop, when you met with your friend. You had had plans to talk about something else, but instead spent the whole time enthralled with their work. Then you can leaf through a few examples of their work and recall how you shared this one, that one, with your friend, and how she laughed at the right places, wanted the phone number to call this or that writer to learn more. The best will be if this is all true! As you do this, bear in mind that the way you read your students' work can make that work seem like a precious jewel. It is especially important to read aloud the writing that your strugglers have made in this same way. Don't ever read it in ways that display the errors and mess-ups—published work should always be fancied up, even if just by the reader!

If your minilesson began that way, you could transition to your teaching point by saying that your friend asked whether the kids were judging only the best work. Did they ever look over all their specimens and determine the least good pieces? That can lead you to say something like, "Today I want to teach you that reviewers, judges, don't always look for the most powerful, the most unusual, the most interesting item. Judges can also look for the least powerful, least unusual, the least interesting item. Sometimes, in a joking and fun way, people talk about this as 'giving the booby prize.' To judge for the booby prize, judges again look at one trait, then another."

If you decide to continue on with the collection of toy dogs you have used before in this unit, your demonstration could have a part in it that goes something like this: "Writers, I want to be sure you realize that sometimes people who are experts on a topic, who collect a lot of information about a topic, write to convince others of what they believe are the worst specimens in their collections. They might write about the worst ballplayer, the worst book, the worst dog. You already know that to do this, the opinion writer needs to produce reasons that back up his or her opinion."

When talking with children about how one goes about judging a collection to identify the worst item in that collection, you will want to remind children that again, the judge needs to provide reasons. You could demonstrate how you awarded one of your dogs with a booby prize, for example. You'll want to return to the idea of examining the contenders for a trait at a time. Say, for example, you examine your dogs for their personality and find that one of the dogs seems so lethargic, so bored with the entire process, that because he shows no enthusiasm, you rank him low in this trait. Or perhaps the dog that is ranked low for personality looks as if he snarls at other dogs, and it is never okay to hurt others. Make sure it's not looks alone that lead to a negative opinion.

The important part of the demonstration is that the point is made that, again, the judge offers multiple reasons and details to support those reasons.

You could, of course, use the active engagement as a time for children to determine their own booby prize winners, but we don't recommend that. This is going to be a lot of fun for children, and they'll do it without needing your support, so we suggest you save that work for when children are back at their seats. Instead, perhaps you can ask children to tell each other what they noticed you doing as a judge. This, then, would give them yet one more chance to talk about evidence-based decisions.

The class might even generate a list of do's and don'ts. You could help them realize that you didn't use words like *ugly* or *mean* to talk about the reasons for your judgment; you instead used words that *were* specific and descriptive.

Your temptation will be to send children off to select their booby prize winner and write why that item is the worst. Certainly children will be eager to do this! Because it will take very little encouragement and support from you for them to do this, you may want to use your link to especially support some of the many the other options that children also have for what they might do today. Remember, the minilessons from prior days should be accumulating, providing children with lots of possible work.

Remind them that they have a lot of different kinds of writing to choose from today—they can write more about their collection, or they can go back to write about a least favorite in their *own* collection. Suggest that choosing a booby prize in someone else's collection could be hurtful, so writers would first need to ask permission. If they have already written several pieces, they could go back to any piece and use the Opinion Writing Checklist to see if they've done all they can do to make their opinion strong and clear. Remind them that they are in charge of their own writing, and they can use all they know about good writing, from this unit and from their whole lives, to make their work today stronger than ever before.

MID-WORKSHOP TEACHING

If you helped one writer to decide that instead of rating items as just good or bad, it was more helpful to rate in more specific ways, you could then highlight that writer's work. Perhaps that writer asked, Which dog looked the happiest? The saddest looking? The most and the least athletic? The fanciest and the plainest? This is yet another opportunity, in another genre of writing, for you to highlight for your students the importance of elaboration in their writing. The genre may change, but the message stays the same.

CONFERRING AND SMALL-GROUP WORK

What will you do on a day like today? The better question is, what *won't* you do? You might decide that today is the perfect opportunity to look across your conferring notes and ask yourself, "Who needs repertoire work? Who, among my writers, tends to rely on one strategy instead of trying different revision strategies?" Most likely, you'll find that you have a clutch of writers who need support doing just that.

You could decide to pull a small-group strategy lesson in which you use demonstration and guided practice to do some assessment-based teaching. Perhaps as you gather that group of students together, you'll also bring the Opinion Writing Checklist and take a couple moments to model for your writers how you consider the different strategies bulleted on the chart, try a few out "in the air," and revise your writing accordingly. As you do this revision work, you may decide to emphasize that you aren't randomly pulling and using strategies, but rather, as you reread your piece, you make decisions based on assessing what is needed. Just as a chef doesn't keep adding one ingredient over and over and over again, but instead adds a dash of one thing, tastes it, then a pinch of something else to balance it out, you'll show students that you, also, need to keep checking out how your piece sounds.

Or, today may be a time to decide which writers continue to believe revision involves using just a tiny caret to add a word. Pull that group together to teach about longer and smarter revisions, encouraging them to use revision strips or entire pages to revise. You might help these writers add revision strips and Post-it notes to a draft, using fancy revision pens if necessary to recruit enthusiasm for revision.

SHARE

For the share today, you might want to select several pieces of writing from which everyone can learn, to talk through with the class.

- Is there a revision strategy that someone used that everyone could benefit from?

- Is there a spelling or conventions strategy that someone used that everyone could use?

- Did someone figure out a new way to make opinion writing stronger?

- Did anyone use their partnership in a way everyone could try?

- Did someone write more than ever before and could that person explain to everyone how?

Enjoy!
Lucy, Celena, and Liz

Bolstering Arguments

IN THIS SESSION, you'll teach students that one way to be more convincing is to ask others who share your opinion to help bolster the argument. It can help to cite the person directly.

GETTING READY

✔ Your own writing about an item in your collection (see Connection, Teaching, and Active Engagement)

✔ "Convince Your Reader!" chart (see Teaching)

✔ Revision tools: Post-it notes, extra pages, sentence strips, revision pens, tape (see Active Engagement)

✔ Student writing folders (see Link)

✔ Students writing folders, pens (see Share)

✔ "How Did I Make My Writing Easy to Read?" chart (see Share)

COMMON CORE STATE STANDARDS: W.1.1, W.1.5, W.2.1, RI1.1, RI.1.8, RFS.1.4, SL.1.1, SL.1.3, L.1.1, L.1.2

FIFTY YEARS AGO, in his now classic *The Process of Education* (1963), Jerome Bruner suggested that "the foundations of any subject may be taught to anybody at any age in some form. There is nothing more central to a discipline than its way of thinking. There is nothing more important in its teaching than to provide the child with the earliest opportunity to learn that way of thinking. . . . In a word, the best introduction to a subject is the subject itself" (76).

This session attempts to give youngsters access to the foundation of argumentation, which is a skill that has received a major spotlight in the Common Core State Standards. It will be many years before children are expected to research the conflicting views held by experts on a topic, sort through the varying claims made by those different experts, and cite directly the arguments that others make. Although it is well beyond reach for a six-year-old to research conflicting views through textual study, it isn't hard for a six-year-old to understand that some kids agree and others disagree with his or her evaluation of action figures, hair bands, or songs. And it is well within reach for the child to begin citing the opinions of others—the child's friend, mother, sister, teacher, principal, or uncle.

Still, this session is more complicated than the earlier ones. It's putting some high demands on children's writing. That is to be expected; it is, after all, almost the last session in this segment of the unit. One of the ways in which you will differentiate your instruction is that once you have recruited all children to engage in work that you know will pay off for them all, you'll then teach in ways that support those who need extra help and that offer horizons for those who need extra challenges. This is one of those sessions that provide extra challenges.

Your minilesson will spark some children to revise, and for those children, it will be helpful if you have a bevy of revision tools at your fingertips during conferring and small-group work. You'll want to be positioned so that you can model and demonstrate revision, using revision strips, extra pages, and Post-it notes. Plan to leave these tools with students so that they can understand that revision is not adding a word with help from a tiny caret . . . it's more.

Bolstering Arguments

CONNECTION

◆ COACHING

Tell about a time when someone disagreed with your opinion in a way that galvanized you to become more convincing.

As the children came to the meeting area today, I slouched in my chair with a sad scowl on my face. As soon as everyone was seated, I began my story, telling it with an exasperated voice, "Yesterday when I got home from school, I was really excited to share my opinion writing with my brother. I was pretty excited to tell him about the best dog in my collection. I read my whole piece to him, like this." I cleared my throat and read in a high and mighty voice:

> I think the retriever is the best dog in my collection!
>
> She's a strong dog with powerful muscles. Her black fur is shiny and smooth. She's got big brown eyes that look at you without looking away. She's a great dog.

"And when I finished reading it to him I said, 'Isn't it great? Don't you agree that the retriever is the best dog in my collection?'" Then, I turned to the boys and girls and asked, "Do you know what he said? He said, 'The retriever? Yuck! If *I* were choosing the best dog, I would definitely *not* choose the boring old retriever! I'd choose a greyhound or a Dalmatian.'

"Well, when he said that, I knew *exactly* what I had to do. I had to revise. I had to try to do a better job explaining my opinion so that he would not think the retriever is boring. I decided to pull out all the stops. Today is our last day writing and revising opinion pieces about our collections, and then we're going to celebrate them. So today, I'm going to show you one way you can pull out all the stops!"

❖ **Name the teaching point.**

"Today I want to teach you that when opinion writers want to pull out all the stops, they sometimes find others who can help them generate even more reasons to support their opinions. They sometimes even refer to—that is, quote—what those other people have said."

The experienced opinion writer supplies reasons to support an opinion with a lot of automaticity, not needing strategies to help him or her do this work. Skilled workers focus on the goal, not the process for reaching the goal. But if someone encounters trouble and needs to learn a new procedure, for a time that person proceeds as if following a new recipe. Okay, so first I hold the yardstick. Like this? Okay, then what?

Because strategies are responses to problems, when you teach kids strategies for improving their writing, you will begin by showing that you encountered a problem, and that led you to set forth to accomplish a challenging goal. In this minilesson, help kids turn rejection into determined effort and, meanwhile, extend their skill base.

TEACHING

Explain that to be more convincing, you sought help from people who agreed with you and helped you think of more reasons to support your opinion.

"Writers, right now I want you to listen to what I did last night, when I wanted to be more convincing, because I think even though you guys are six years old, you might be able to do some of this very grown-up work. You ready? Be researchers, studying what I did so that you can maybe do these things too."

I checked that the children seemed ready to notice what I was doing. "Okay, so I knew that opinion writers sometimes go to others who feel as they do and say, 'Help me make a strong argument.' So I thought to myself, 'Who can help me be more convincing?' And then I had it! I thought about how my mom has always been a fan of retrievers. I phoned her up (I held an imaginary phone). I explained that I need help being more convincing, and she didn't hesitate a moment before saying (and I acted out my mother's voice), 'One thing you can tell your brother is that it only takes a retriever about one hour to fall totally in love with a new person. They're so friendly that they'll follow anyone, anywhere. You could never tell a retriever not to talk to strangers.' She added, 'The only thing they love more than people is food.'

"What do you think about adding a paragraph where I quote my mother saying retrievers love people?" I said. The children agreed that would help. "Right now, think in your mind of what exactly I might write," I said.

After giving a moment of silence for children to think about how the new information could get incorporated into my writing, I continued. "I wanted some information from an expert, so I also phoned Rachel Hill who breeds retrievers. She said, 'The great thing about them is they are working dogs. They will go anywhere to retrieve ducks. Even if a lake is almost frozen, retrievers will dive right in.'

"I realized I could put that detail into my writing by putting in the exact words that the breeder said: 'Rachel Hill, who breeds these dogs, says 'Even if the lakes are almost frozen, retrievers will dive right in.' Do you think that would help convince my brother?" I asked the children.

ACTIVE ENGAGEMENT

Give students an opportunity to come up with additional information to be added to your writing while you model revising using various revision tools.

"Let's see if you can help me add even more to this writing. While I write some of this in, will you and your partner talk with another partnership and see if any one of you knows something *else* we could say about why retrievers—any kind of retrievers—are great dogs?" I said, my voice trailing off as I knew full well that in a class of twenty-eight kids, more than a few were apt to have experience with America's most popular dog.

I know, I know, I went overboard quoting my mother, but remember we've chosen the topic of dogs because it's one I know well, and this is exactly what my mother would say had I asked her to defend retrievers (which are not actually her favorite). When there is a ring of truth coming through in our teaching, kids hear that authenticity.

When students are in sixth grade, they are expected to begin to think about the warrant behind different people's claims. Someone who breeds retrievers has a different authority— and different bias—than someone else. I'm not explaining to children now that it's important to add details about a source, but I do illustrate best practices.

I quickly turned to the piece of writing and began to add onto it, writing my new sentences first on a revision strip, and then attaching the strip to my writing. The children joined into a shared reading of the new text.

> I think the retriever is the best dog in my collection!
>
> She's a strong dog with powerful muscles. Her black fur is shiny and smooth. She's got big brown eyes that look at you without looking away. She's a great dog.
>
> My mother thinks that retrievers are so friendly they will follow anyone, anywhere. It hardly takes them any time to adopt a new person as their BFF. They love people almost as much as they love food.
>
> "They are happy to retrieve for you," Rachel Hill, who breeds these dogs, says. "Even if a lake is almost frozen, retrievers will dive right in."

As we reached the ending of it, I asked, "Do any of you have something else I can add?" Several hands shot up. Ashley spoke first: "They sleep with you?" she said. "Can that go in?" I said, "Is that really true?" and Ashley nodded emphatically, explaining that her cousin had one until the dog died, and the dog always slept with her cousin. I promised to add that information after the minilesson was over.

Debrief in ways that spotlight the ways the work you and the children have done to make one piece of writing more convincing could also make other pieces of writing more convincing.

"So writers, have you have learned new ways to make writing convincing?" I asked.

"Now there's real facts about those dogs so it's like it's teaching you about it, and if it's real facts then people have to just listen because it's true," Monique asserted. I nodded. "It is wise to revise your opinion pieces by getting the help from others who agree with you. They can help you add information in ways that make your opinion pieces even more convincing. You can even quote their exact words."

LINK

Ask students to reread their writing and make a plan for how to make it stronger, all the while providing a drumroll for the upcoming celebration.

"Writers, the important thing right now is that you have just one more day to make all of the writing you have been doing so far in this unit more convincing. Right now, will you read through all the work you have done so far and think about who in this classroom might help you make your arguments more convincing?" I gave children a minute to do that rereading while they sat in the meeting area. Then I said, "I bet that as you reread, you found some pieces of writing that aren't done or that don't have very many reasons. Will you give me a thumbs up if *you*, even without help, could make some of your writing more convincing?" Most children agreed, and so I sent them off to work.

If the children can't talk to their partners for as long as it takes you to write this, then recruit them to dictate as you write. Or ask them to read what you have written aloud to their partner and talk about the techniques they're learning that they could try in their writing. Meanwhile, write quickly!

In an instance like this, it is likely that five kids will have ideas for ways to contribute to the text. Not a lot is gained by hearing one after another after another add onto the text. Learn to watch your clock and to protect time for children to work on their own writing, even if that means not always hearing from every last contributor. You can always say, "I'll leave the marker here and during writing time, add more to this!"

This again is a place where you can't call on every contributor. Ten minutes are probably up, and it is time for kids to get going on their writing.

Using Small-Group Work to Provide Follow-Up to the Minilesson

N O MATTER HOW CLEAR AND FOCUSED YOUR TEACHING, no matter how many opportunities your students are given to try out a new strategy during the active engagement portion of your minilesson, it is not uncommon that you may have a handful of students or perhaps more who will need additional support with the new strategy. If you notice that there is a significant portion of your class needing another go, you may decide to reteach your minilesson on a subsequent day. If it is a smaller portion, you may decide to pull a small group together and reteach the minilesson that way. The link portion of your minilesson is a good time to do this kind of quick assessment.

MID-WORKSHOP TEACHING **Using Quotation Marks to Show Dialogue**

"Writers," I said, "pens down and eyes up." I waited a moment until I was sure each child's eyes were on me before I began. "I can see that many of you are writing to make your pieces *more* persuasive, and one way you're doing that is by asking others what they know and then writing what they say. Remember, way back when you were writing Small Moments and you 'unfroze' your characters, you were careful to make sure you let readers know what those characters were saying by adding quotation marks around their talking. You'll need to do that same work when you write what people say about your topics. Look at Jorge's writing" I said, as I held up his piece (see Figure 6–1). "He just added the words, 'Rosa says that Spiderman is the coolest color.' Jorge was getting ready to make sure he made Rosa's words belong to her by adding quotation marks around them. He put the left curly quotation around where Rosa's words start, right here—'Spiderman.' Then, he put the right curly quotation where Rosa's words ended, here—'color.' That's important, writers. When you revise your pieces to make them more persuasive, and if you put in what someone says to you, you have to make sure their words belong to them by adding those curly quotations. Put the left curly quotation where the talking starts, and the right curly quotation where the talking ends. Keep writing!" I rallied and continued to confer and coach writers.

> Spider man is best. He has no cape but he has web shooters.
> He has sticky feet and big muscles. Rosa like Spiderman
> too. Rosa say "Spiderman is good color."

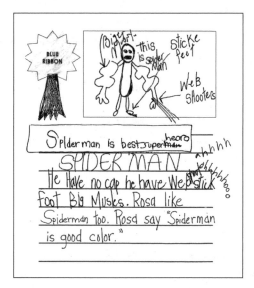

FIG. 6–1   Jorge edited his piece to include quotation marks to cite his source directly.

I gathered a small group for additional work on pulling out all the stops, using a piece of my own writing that I had enlarged on chart paper. I asked students to bring their writing folders so that they could begin writing as soon as I was done teaching. "Writers, I have my own writing here; I am hoping that we can work together to make my piece about the playground even more convincing. Let's be sure to pull out all the stops to make sure others agree with us. First, let's read it together," I said, as I touched the first word on the line and waited for voices to join in:

> I like everything on the playground, but the best thing on the playground is the slide.
>
> I notice that many kids love it the most!
>
> They love to climb up the pole on the end of the slide.
>
> You can slide down forward or backward.
>
> It is so fun that we want to play on it all day long!

"We know that one way to make our opinion writing even more convincing is to find friends to help us and think, 'Who else agrees that the slide is the best thing at the playground? What expert information can we add to teach people about this?'

"Hmm . . . I'm wondering who in this group agrees that the slide really *is* the best thing at the playground." I tapped my chin as I scanned the students sitting at the table. A slew of arms shot up in fervent agreement. "Well, it seems that we have a lot of friends to help us make this more convincing. Right now, think to yourself, 'What do I know about the slide at the playground that might be important information to teach people?'

"Imagine that someone came into our room and read our writing and said, 'The slide? Blech! That boring thing? The slide is definitely *not* the coolest thing.' What might you say to convince him to agree with us? What expert information could we add to make others feel the way we do?" I gave students a moment to think and then signaled for them to share their ideas with friends at the table.

The group was alive with chatter. I listened in with a revision pen and large Post-it notes in hand, ready to collect pieces of information as partners shared.

Caleb said, "We could add, 'The slide is bigger.' It is! It's the biggest one! It's bigger than the swings. I mean higher." I quickly recorded Caleb's fact on a Post-it note.

I moved on to listen in to others in time to hear Jorge say, "The slide is safe for babies." Again, I recorded this information.

"It's really cool. It's not boring at all because it's a spiral and it has a tunnel. It's almost like you're on a roller coaster!" Aubry exclaimed emphatically. I jotted this down before calling the students back together.

"Wow, if anyone ever comes into our classroom and tries to disagree, you'll have *lots* to say back about this topic. I listened in as you were talking, and you each had so many smart ideas and expert information about the slide that I think will be important to add to our piece."

I stuck each Post-it note up on my piece as I read each addition aloud, giving a nod to the students from whom I had collected these revisions:

> The slide is the biggest thing at the park. It's even higher than the swings!

"That's convincing," I said to the group. "That's expert information."

> Don't worry, the slide is safe for babies, too.

"Even more convincing!" I said, delighted.

> And some people might say it's boring, but it's really cool because it has a spiral and a tunnel. It feels like you're on a roller coaster!

"Oh, and that one talks right back to anyone who might say the slide is boring to prove that it's not boring at all! Nicely done!" I remarked.

"Wow, look at all the stops you pulled out to revise and make the playground piece more convincing. Now when people read it, they have even more reasons to agree with us. I bet you'll find ways to do this in your own writing, too! We revised all over the page, and we even added pages. We wrote expert information. We talked back to our readers. We wrote detailed information, too! As I restated each strategy we'd used to make our writing more convincing, I touched the revisions we'd made. Then I looked at the students' work sitting in front of them, waiting to be revised.

"Now think about how you can do this sort of work in your opinion pieces. In fact, get your writing out now, while we are here together, and check your writing to see if it looks and sounds like the writing we just did together. We pulled out all the stops just now when we wrote together. Now do some of that in your piece. First reread, then go back and pull out all the stops." Once students were well on their way, I moved on from the group and began conferring with others.

Fixing Up Writing to Ensure It Is Easy to Read

Ask students to reread the opinion pieces in their folders, checking for readability.

I called writers to the meeting area, asking everyone to bring their folders and writing pens and sit beside their writing partner on the rug. "Tomorrow we will be having our first celebration of this unit! Very exciting stuff. I bet you all can't wait to read each other's writing; I know I can't! But before you share your writing with others, you will want to go back to it and make sure that you have made it easy to read. Sometimes when writers make lots of revisions and add more and more to their writing, some parts end up not sounding quite right! Some parts might not make sense. I want to remind you how important it is to reread your pieces to find parts that are not quite clear and fix up those parts so readers will understand exactly what you want to say. Reread, pointing under each word. And as you reread your own writing, think about and use what you know to make your writing easy to read. If you need to, use the chart that we've made together to remember all the ways we can make our writing easy to read."

I gestured to the chart we'd constructed across the year, starting with the very first unit of study, and touched each bullet as I reminded the students of all they already know.

"As you reread, do a self-check and make sure each and every page is easy for your readers to read, and follow through by doing what you need to do to make writing readable. If you are stuck or confused about something, you are sitting right next to your partner. Use them! Ready, go!"

As the students read through the writing in their folders, I circulated, paying compliments to writers who were rereading each page, touching each word, checking for lower- and uppercase letters, and editing for end punctuation.

Celebrations weave across this book, marking the end of every bend, rather than once at the end of the unit. This allows writers ongoing opportunities for self-assessment, revision, and editing. Fixing up their pieces from this first bend and drawing upon a growing repertoire of editing strategies will propel the work students collect across the next bend.

How Did I Make My Writing Easy to Read?

- I put spaces between my words.
- I checked the word wall.
- I spelled tricky words the best I can.
- I reread my writing, touching each word.
- I used capital letters at the beginning of sentences.
- I used capital letters for names.
- I used different sorts of end punctuation.

Session 7

Editing and Publishing

Making Writing "Best in Show"!

TODAY IS THE FIRST OF THREE publishing and celebration days during this unit. As you draw this first bend to a close, preparing for the mini-celebration, you will rally students to reread and edit *all* the opinion pieces they've created so far, from the first opinion piece they penned at the beginning of the unit, to the one they just started yesterday. A day like today involves big work, and you'll want to be sure to double-check that the writing center is well stocked with revision strips and extra pages, as well as pens for revising and editing. You'll make sure that your staplers are full of staples and your staple removers are staple free, ready for pulling apart and rearranging.

"Students need a session to sit back, take in, fix up, and celebrate their opinions."

Students need a session to sit back, take in, fix up, and celebrate their opinions. Today's session is tailored for that to happen. It's a day to teach your writers that they gain power by making their pieces as readable as possible.

The Common Core State Standards expect first-grade students to demonstrate a command of the conventions of standard English grammar and usage when writing or speaking. Additionally, it's expected that first-grade students demonstrate command of conventions of standard English capitalization, punctuation, and spelling when writing. First-grade students are expected to print all upper- and lowercase letters in words and sentences, produce complete simple and compound sentences, capitalize proper nouns, and use end punctuation. While writing workshop allows for application of this work every day, taking today as a special "get ready time" can only benefit the students. What's more, you'll be

IN THIS SESSION, you'll teach students that writers often use checklists to make their writing the best that it can be.

GETTING READY

✔ "How Did I Make My Writing Easy to Read?" chart (see Teaching and Active Engagement)

✔ Opinion Writing Checklist, Grades 1 and 2 (see Teaching and Active Engagement)

✔ Children's folders with past work

✔ Revision tools such as Post-it notes, extra pages, sentence strips, revision pens, tape, staplers, and staple removers in the writing center

✔ Blue ribbons (we suggest a bag of bows from your local dollar store) (see Share)

COMMON CORE STATE STANDARDS: W.1.1, W.1.5, W.2.1, RFS.1.1, RFS.1.4, SL.1.1, SL.1.6, L.1.1, L.1.2

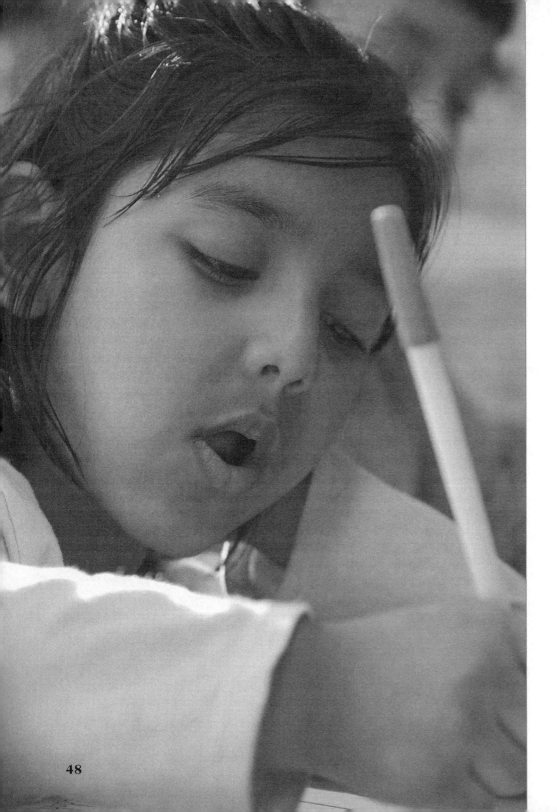

amazed with the way writers touch and read each word carefully, both independently and with a partner, to make decisions about the letters they are constructing and punctuation they are practicing.

Today's session ends with a "mini-celebration" to help students realize the ways in which this hard editing work pays off. During the share, you'll have students come together in small groups, read two or three of their pieces, and compliment each other. You'll want to make sure your charts from the unit are on display and accessible for students, so that the compliments children grant one another will directly reflect the language and strategies from the unit.

One last suggestion you may consider is to prepare (or have children make) judging paddles, much like those used during competitions to hold up bold numbers awarding final scores. Every paddle will read "10," and your writers will use these to silently praise the work of their peers, as each writer proudly, and formally, puts her piece into the class writing gallery. These can be as fancy as a craft stick and circle of card stock, or as simple as a sheet of paper with a giant "10" printed on one side.

Editing and Publishing
Making Writing "Best in Show"!

CONNECTION

Rally writers to prepare all of their writing for the upcoming "Best in Show" celebration.

"Writers, ever since we started this unit, you have worked really hard to review and rank things you know well—stickers, books, Barbies, model cars, coins. You are the expert on your collection, and so you have taught the rest of us about what makes for a really good Barbie, a really good action figure, a really good yo-yo.

"Today is the very last day in this part of our unit. After this you are going to use your skills at reviewing and judging in a new way. But before we end our work with your collections, I think you need to do one more competition. This time, instead of entering your toy dogs or your Barbies in a competition, I'm hoping you will enter—you ready for this?—*your writing* in a competition. I'm hoping you will choose two or three of your best pieces of writing and then lay them out beside your collection. Then we'll send some judges around, only this time they won't be judging the stuff that you brought—they'll be judging your writing to help you choose the writing that is your best. After the judges help you decide which is your best piece of writing, they'll give one piece of your writing a blue 'Best in Show' ribbon, and you can later decide whether you agree."

It makes sense to transfer all that students have learned about judging and defending judgments to a new collection: their writing. This is a natural extension of all they've done so far.

Offer an analogy that compares participants in a competition with writers.

"You may not know this, but during the Westminster Dog Show, before the 'Best in Show' event, the judges give the dog handlers time to go backstage and prepare the dogs for the final event. The dog handlers put the dogs up on a table, and they comb every single strand of hair on the dog. They look into the dogs' eyes and make sure they are clear and clean. They check the dogs' teeth and ears. They even take time to make tiny little clips between the dogs' toenails. Let me tell you, they do *every* single thing they can to make sure it has the *best* possible chance of winning first place. No detail is too small. Everything they know how to do, they do it, right up until the very last second.

Notice that usually a single text or topic threads through many of the minilessons. In this instance, my dog collection provides cohesion to this bend in the unit.

"I think today is your day to be like those dog handlers, but instead of readying dogs, you are going to do all that you know to get all of your writing ready for the celebration tomorrow. Today is your day to take your writing and go over each and every piece to prepare. To do this, you'll need to rely on *everything* you know about strong opinion writing, as well as use all the tools we have in our classroom to revise and edit your pieces to make them their very best. Today you will get *all* of your pieces ready, and then you will read your choices to others, and they'll award your 'Best in Show'!"

"Today, I want to teach you that one way to make sure your writing is the best that it can be is to use the checklists that are used to judge writing as To-Do lists, reminding you of all that you want to do to make your writing the best that it can be."

TEACHING AND ACTIVE ENGAGEMENT

Rally students to survey their environment—the classroom—collecting any resources that can help them judge their own writing and can help them know ways to improve their writing.

"Will you study the room for a minute and give me a thumbs up when you see a tool or a chart that helps *you* to do your best editing and fancying up of your writing?"

Thumbs immediately went up. Jorge said, "Word walls help me check words!" "Yeah, and the 'How Did I Make My Writing Easy to Read?' chart!" added Bradley. "The Opinion Writing Checklist," Skylee said, racing to it. "Yes," I added, "of course!" I moved the charts front and center.

LINK

Send writers off with the reminder that charts can become To-Do lists.

"Writers, just like the people at the Westminster Dog Show take time to make their dogs perfect, you are going to want to take time to make each piece of your writing as perfect as it can be. Use the checklists around our classroom as To-Do lists, reminding you of hopes that people have for your writing. After you finish improving one piece of writing, don't wait! Move quickly to the next, and improve that piece until you make sure *all* of your writing is ready to share!"

Opinion Writing Checklist

	Grade 1	NOT YET	STARTING TO	YES!	Grade 2	NOT YET	STARTING TO	YES!
	Structure				**Structure**			
Overall	I wrote my opinion or my likes and dislikes and said why.	☐	☐	☐	I wrote my opinion or my likes and dislikes and gave reasons for my opinion.	☐	☐	☐
Lead	I wrote a beginning in which I got readers' attention. I named the topic or text I was writing about and gave my opinion.	☐	☐	☐	I wrote a beginning in which I not only gave my opinion, but also set readers up to expect that my writing would try to convince them of it.	☐	☐	☐
Transitions	I said more about my opinion and used words such as *and* and *because*.	☐	☐	☐	I connected parts of my piece using words such as *also*, *another*, and *because*.	☐	☐	☐
Ending	I wrote an ending for my piece.	☐	☐	☐	I wrote an ending in which I reminded readers of my opinion.	☐	☐	☐
Organization	I wrote a part where I got readers' attention and a part where I said more.	☐	☐	☐	My piece had different parts; I wrote a lot of lines for each part.	☐	☐	☐
	Development				**Development**			
Elaboration	I wrote at least one reason for my opinion.	☐	☐	☐	I wrote at least two reasons and wrote at least a few sentences about each one.	☐	☐	☐
Craft	I used labels and words to give details.	☐	☐	☐	I chose words that would make readers agree with my opinion.	☐	☐	☐
	Language Conventions				**Language Conventions**			
Spelling	I used all I knew about words and chunks of words (*at*, *op*, *it*, etc.) to help me spell.	☐	☐	☐	To spell a word, I used what I knew about spelling patterns (*tion*, *er*, *ly*, etc.).	☐	☐	☐
	I spelled all the word wall words right and used the word wall to help me spell other words.	☐	☐	☐	I spelled all of the word wall words correctly and used the word wall to help me figure out how to spell other words.	☐	☐	☐

How Did I Make My Writing Easy to Read?

- I put spaces between my words.
- I checked the word wall.
- I spelled tricky words the best I can.
- I reread my writing, touching each word.
- I used capital letters at the beginning of sentences.
- I used capital letters for names.
- I used different sorts of end punctuation.

Using a Variety of Punctuation Marks

THIS DAY IS A GOOD TIME for you to focus on one-on-one conferring. As you confer with writers around conventions of writing, remember to look for what is there, rather than what is not there. It's important to teach using children's strengths.

Listen to how a writer reads her piece aloud. If you hear her pause in places that haven't been marked with commas or periods, help her add the appropriate punctuation. It may be quick coaching the first few times, followed by a gradual release of your support, allowing the writer to approximate these punctuation decisions, to decide independently where the commas, exclamation points, periods, and question marks belong.

I sat down beside Gabriel as he read over his piece (see Figure 7–1). I glanced over his shoulder to follow along, taking the time to quickly assess notable strengths, as well as possibilities for teaching. It was clear that Gabriel was aware of punctuation, and had inserted periods in several places across his writing. He had also included capitals at the start of each new sentence. However, I noticed that he had not varied his punctuation across his piece, strictly using periods to mark each sentence. And so, I started in on the conference.

John Cena is the B-E-S-T of all the wrestlers even better than ones that are not in my collection. He is best because he is strong and powerful! He always beats the bad guys! His muscles stronger and bigger then Canes muscles.

John Cena has cool wrestling clothes. One way his clothes are cool is because he doesn't wear wrestler shorts he wears jean shorts. Another way is he wears basketball shoes when he wrestles. Other wrestlers don't wear basketball shoes.

John Cena knows how to do a lot of good moves. One of his best moves is the attitude adjustment. When he does the attitude

adjustment on other guys he says his catch phrase. His catch phrase is You can't see me! One night I wrestled with my dad. I pretended I was John Cena and I yelled You can't see me! really slow and jumped at my dad. But I didn't really hurt him. My dad was Hulk Hogan when we played and he was funny.

Hulk Hogan is an old-fashioned wrestler. But we were just pretending.

MID-WORKSHOP TEACHING   Using Writing Partners as a Final Check before Publication

I stopped children as they worked independently, and when I had their attention, I began, "You are all so busy at work to get your pieces ready for our celebration, making sure all of your writing is the very best it can be! When handlers are putting the finishing touches on their dogs just before the show, they sometimes ask a friend to give the dog one last look to make sure they haven't missed anything—even a single hair out of place! Writers can do the same thing. You can borrow the eyes and ears of your partner to help find something you may have forgotten to do. This way, your pieces are sure to be their absolute best!

"Will you team up with your writing partner? Partner 1 will start first. Put the piece you're working on right now between you, and read it out loud to your partner. Then, together, decide what *else* you might need to do to make your writing even better. Remember, you can use the charts in the classroom to remind you of all the strategies you already know to make your pieces more convincing and easy to read."

① John Cena is the B-E-S-T of all the Wreslers even better than ones that are not in my Collection. He is Best because he is strong and power full! He allways beats the Bad guys! His Muscles

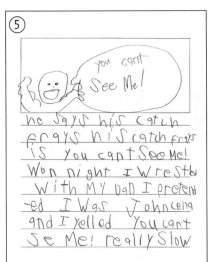

② Stronger and Bigger then canes Muscles John Cena has cool Wrestling cloths. one way his cloths are cool is Because he Dosnt wore Wrestler shorts he Whears

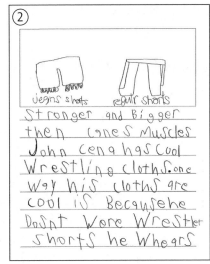

③ Jeans shorts another way is he wears Basket Ball shoes When he Wrestles. Other Wrestlers Dont Where Basket Ball shoes.

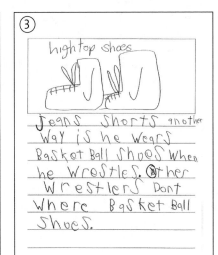

④ John Cena knows how to do a lot of good Moves one of his Best moves is the attitude ajutment. Wen he does the attitude ajustment on other guys

⑤ he says his catch frays his catch frays is you cant see me! Won night I wresteld with my Dad I pretend-ed I was John cena and I yelled You cant Se Me! really Slow

⑥ and Jumped at My Dad But I DiDNT really hurt him. My Dad was Hulk Hogen When We played and he was funny. Hulk Hogen is an old Fashoned Wrestler

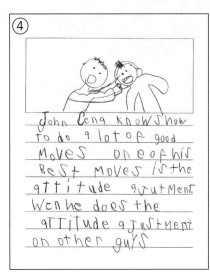

⑦ But We were Just Pretending.

FIG. 7–1   Gabriel edited his piece to include varied punctuation to reflect how the writing should sound when read aloud.

"Hi, Gabriel! Can I stop you for just a bit?" Then, I began with a compliment, highlighting a particular strength with specificity: "I'd really like to compliment you about something so smart that you do as a writer. I notice that at the end of almost all of your sentences, you remembered to use a punctuation mark. You put a period here, and here, and over here. That way, your readers will know to take a stop." I pointed across Gabriel's page to uncover the evidence of this skill. "Plus, you even remembered to start every new sentence with a capital letter. Extra smart!" Gabriel smiled broadly, bursting with pride. Meanwhile, nearby students peered over, their ears perking up to the awarded praise. This would surely disperse the teaching value of my compliment to neighboring writers.

"Can I teach you another way you can use punctuation to help your reader know how you want your piece to sound? You can read your writing out loud and listen to how your voice changes as you read the words. Then, you can include not only periods but exclamation points, question marks, and even quotation marks to show that somebody is talking. Try that now: read your piece out loud, and listen for places when your voice stops or changes." I gestured for Gabriel to start from the top, reading line by line.

As he paused after the first sentence, I tapped on the period he had already included and gave a thumbs-up signal. Then, as Gabriel read with extra excitement, skipping past a sentence punctuated by a period, I coached in. "When you just read this part, this is how your voice changed a bit." I moved on to echo, "'He *always* beats the bad guys!' What kind of mark would be best to use so that your reader will change their voice the same way?"

"An exclamation point!" Gabriel affirmed. I smiled and nodded and tapped on the page to nudge him to edit. After doing so, he continued reading aloud.

As he read the final sentence, changing his voice to mimic the wrestler, I prompted him to go back and reread. "Read that part once more, and listen really closely to what happens to your voice."

Gabriel echoed back, "His catchphrase is, 'You *can't* see me!'" Then, he quickly turned to make a fast edit, changing the period to an exclamation point.

"So, Gabriel, these words up here," I said, pointing to the speech bubble in his picture, "is what John Cena says?"

"Yup! He says it all the time to the guys he wrestles."

"I like how you put the words in your speech bubble down here in your sentence. You can use quotation marks around those same words to show your reader that someone is talking."

"Oh yeah, just like in my *Froggy* books," Gabriel connected, recalling observations about punctuation he had made as a reader.

"Exactly, just like the author of the *Froggy* books made sure to include all kinds of punctuation, like quotation marks, you can add them to your writing to show parts with talking," I reminded.

Before moving on to meet with another student, I restated the strategy to support transfer across all of Gabriel's work, as a writer. "So, Gabriel, whenever you are writing or editing your work, remember to listen to changes in your voice as your read your piece aloud. Then, be sure to include *all kinds* of punctuation that will help your readers know *exactly* how you want your writing to sound." Then, I prompted Gabriel to continue this practice across the remaining pieces in his folder. "I bet you could make the rest of your writing even better by reading those pieces and fixing up the punctuation! Go for it!"

Celebrating Student Writing

In small groups, give students an opportunity to share their pieces for publication. Students can then provide feedback and award blue ribbons to the best piece.

I called students over to the meeting area, asking each child to bring two or three pieces that they had spent the most time preparing for publication and to sit in small groups of three or four children.

"It's time to present your pieces!" I said, the excitement building in my voice. "Decide who will go first, then read your 'Best in Show' contenders to your group. Then, groups, you can award your blue ribbon to the piece you thought was best! Groups, remember to be sure to tell the writer the reasons *why* you think the piece is the best. You'll probably want to use our writing charts to give really great compliments!" I prompted, gesturing toward the strategy charts that lined the meeting area.

As the children began the celebration share circles, I moved from group to group, keeping readers on track and making sure that *all* writers had a chance to share their writing. I whispered in to supply needed support, reminding writers to speak audibly and clearly and helping students grant specific compliments to supply reasons for why they think one piece was best when awarding a "Best in Show" ribbon. I reminded students to look toward the charts, as I moved from group to group, helping writers articulate the specific details they noticed in each other's writing, to reinforce these skills and strategies in the work they'll continue to do as writers across the unit.

After about ten minutes (we know it is a little bit long for a share—but worth it!), I gathered the class back into one big circle and formally called each writer's name as he or she placed the piece into the writing gallery. As each writer moved toward front of the class, inserting their piece into their gallery pocket, I led the students in lifting their judging paddles to display their perfect "10s" into the air, celebrating the impressive work each child had done.

You'll want to encourage children to name specific strategies their classmates used in their writing as a means of reinforcing this work as they move into the next bend of the unit. When students can articulate their process, it strengthens their ability to apply it independently.

Writing Reviews to Persuade Others

IN THIS SESSION, you'll teach students that review writers write not only to share their opinion but also to persuade others to share their opinion. Writers can study mentor texts to learn the best ways to do that.

GETTING READY

✔ Posters or pictures from well-known movies (see Connection)

✔ Several menus from local restaurants (see Connection)

✔ Several video game cartridges with the titles visible (see Connection)

✔ "Thinking Outside the Box" chart (see Connection and Share)

✔ "Convince Your Reader!" anchor chart (see Guided Inquiry)

✔ Mentor reviews of a game, movie, or retaurant—an enlarged copy as well as individual copies for students (see Guided Inquiry)

✔ Post-it notes (see Guided Inquiry)

✔ Chart paper, marker (see Guided Inquiry and Share)

✔ Opinion Writing Checklists, Grade 1 and Grade 2 (see Conferring and Small-Group Work)

✔ Tiny topic notepads for each student (see Share)

COMMON CORE STATE STANDARDS: W.1.1, W.1.7; RI.1.1, RI.1.8; SL.1.1; L.1.1, L.1.2, L.1.6

FROM THE FIRST DAY OF SCHOOL, children arrive at your door, carrying with them symbols that proclaim, "This is who I am. This is what I love"—backpacks and folders revealing favorite video games, pop stars, and sports teams; notebooks plastered with stickers of superheroes and cartoon characters; even lunchboxes and T-shirts, proudly sharing much-loved television shows and movies. These initial markers of distinction with which children identify give words to the joys and interests each student holds dear. From the beginning of this unit, you've invited students to share personal collections, clearing shelves, corners, and tables for shoebox treasures, and ultimately, clearing a path to help children find words to express themselves through writing.

As students closely examined their prized possessions to formulate opinions and write in ways that express these feelings—holding up baseball cards, toy soldiers, and friendship bracelets, twisting each slowly in the light to study every facet before deciding on the most prized, and least coveted—you've planted the seeds for the work writers will now do as they move on to persuasive reviews. During the first bend, you helped writers understand ways to make their opinions clear and compelling, supporting their claims with reasons, examples, and important information. As you now move into the second bend of this unit, the focus shifts ever so slightly, channeling children to sharpen their skills of persuasion as they write to captivate readers with reviews of movies, video games, restaurants, vacation spots, and more. While opinion writing still fuels the work students will do, it is the art of persuasion that bubbles to the surface, building upon the strategies writers have already learned.

Starting today, you'll remind children to bring all they now know about opinion writing and to now investigate ways to incorporate craft (with an emphasis on elaboration and structure) while writing persuasive reviews. As the bend unfolds, students will learn to compose pieces, not only with clearly stated opinions, reasons, and ranks but also with specific examples, relevant information, tucked anecdotes, recommendations, and catchy introductions and conclusions.

To support this shift, we suggest you use a couple of published reviews to help students get a sense of the structure, language, voice, and topics used by review writers. By leading your class on an inquiry study of these selected mentor reviews, you'll guide children to unearth strategies for writing persuasively, adding new and challenging strategies for opinion writing to the repertoire they've already developed. You'll address several of these strategies across this bend, providing explicit demonstrations to help children engage in this challenging work.

"The art of persuasion bubbles to the surface, building upon the strategies writers have already learned."

You'll first guide children to generate topics for the reviews they'll soon write. Allow children to make choices freely about the subject they will review, offering a menu of topics, such as restaurants, video games, music, movies, television shows, amusement parks, and the like. This freedom of choice allows students to conduct the more sophisticated work of teaching important information, sharing anecdotes of personal experiences, as well as including suggestions, warnings, and recommendations in their reviews. You may question the fact that we aren't highlighting reviews of books or magazines. This will be the focus of the final bend in the unit. We recommend that you reserve the work for then.

Writing Reviews to Persuade Others

CONNECTION

Pique the students' interest in a new type of opinion writing by telling them that there are people whose job it is to play video games and to eat at restaurants—these are review writers.

Students made their way to the rug, pointing, whispering, and giggling as they took in the video game cartridges that lined the chalk ledge, the movie posters that were taped up on the white board, and the restaurant menus hanging from magnetic clips. Many made comments like, "Oh! I love that movie!" or "My brother has that game!" or "My mom goes to that restaurant," as they made their way to the meeting area.

Once everyone had settled, I leaned forward in my seat as if ready to share the juiciest secret of all time. "What I'm about to tell you may knock your socks off, but I promise it is the absolute truth. Did you know that there are people in this world—maybe one of them lives in your neighborhood—whose *job* it is to play video games or to watch new movies? There are people who get paid money to have dinner in different restaurants or to read the newest books! Really, it's true. These people are called *reviewers*—they write. Their job is to try out different types of things and write about it to share their opinions.

"Take a look at some of the topics that review writers have written reviews about," I said, gesturing toward the display of posters, video games, and restaurant menus. "None of *these* topics could fit inside a shoebox collection—the writers had to go out into the world and actually play the game, or watch the movie, or eat at the restaurant to decide if they loved something and why. Then they wrote reviews to convince people to try what they liked or to stay away from things they didn't like."

Explain that to be review writers, people need to know how to write in support of their opinions, as students have been doing, and they also need to know how to persuade, which may pose new challenges.

"This is the kind of writing you'll be doing for the rest of our unit. *You* will be review writers." I put both my hands in front of me. "On the *one* hand," I explained, acting as though there was a heavy pile of stuff weighing my hand down, "you already know a whole lot about this sort of writing. You are full of opinions and reasons, and you know how to support those opinions with reasons." I gestured toward the "Convince Your Reader!" chart up on the easel. "But, on the *other* hand," I added, holding my other hand out as I switched sides, "review writers have the big job of not *only*

◆ COACHING

The excitement that you bring to today's mini-lesson will set the stage for children. Don't shy away from bringing in reviews that reflect your interests, the movies you love watching, the restaurants you enjoy frequenting. When children witness your excitement, they'll be quick to mirror it with their own.

stating an opinion and supplying reasons but *also* of persuading others. They need to get people they don't even know to trust their judgments and follow their lead.

"Just like review writers all around the world, you can choose to write about things you know and love." I began to voice over a menu of possibilities: "Games, movies, toys, restaurants, cartoons, vacation places . . ." I trailed off as children deliberated. "Show me a thumb when you've got an idea for your first review."

Once I saw that the youngsters had chosen topics, I prompted them to share. "Will you take that idea and pluck it from your brain? Okay, now hold it carefully in your hands like a firefly. Don't let it go! Now, quietly, will you let your partner peek inside at your idea? Whisper to each other what you'll review first." I listened in to a few partnerships to gauge the variety of topics students had selected.

"Such exciting topics!" I remarked. "And today and this week, I will help you learn to write reviews that do those topics justice, that are *especially* convincing. I have a couple of reviews, right here, that I found on the Internet last night. I was on the computer in search of the perfect birthday present for my nephew. He's turning six soon! It was hard for me to decide what to get him. But luckily, there were reviews written by real-life review writers to help me decide. Let's study these reviews together to learn ways *we* can write reviews that are so convincing, readers might follow *our* lead."

TEACHING AND ACTIVE ENGAGEMENT

Name a question that will guide the class inquiry. In this case, "What do review writers do to convince readers to agree?"

"This means that today, I am not teaching you something. Instead, we'll investigate together, just like detectives, to find some answers to this big question, 'What important parts do writers make sure to include to make their reviews so convincing?' Then, we'll be able to ask, 'How can we do this in our reviews, too?'"

GUIDED INQUIRY

Set up writers to investigate mentor reviews by guiding them through a series of steps that help students discover answers to the overarching question.

"Okay, writers, the first thing we'll need to do is to find places in this review that we think are well written. Right now, I am going to read the first review about a board game called Rush Hour: Traffic Jam, and when you hear a part that makes you think, 'I want to write that well,' stick one of your Post-it notes right next to that part, on your copy."

When studying learning progressions in argument writing, we've found that an important consideration in persuasive writing is "social appeal." A writer needs to think about his or her particular audience, and use knowledge of psychology and human nature and rhetoric to coax the audience to think and feel whatever the writer has in mind. First-graders can only begin to do this complicated work—but any six-year-old has already begun to learn tricks to convince adults to say yes to such things as later bedtimes or extra snacks. The same skills are needed now!

Keep in mind that inquiry work is challenging work. You may decide to repeat the inquiry question a time or two as well as gesture to the question at the top of the chart. It may be that you have the writers read the question with you, emphasizing the what in the question so that children understand today they are looking for multiple strategies, not one "right answer."

Feel free to use the mentor reviews that we have crafted, or to find your own online. If you have a whiteboard you may decide to show the mentor review that way, in order to expose students to ways in which the Internet has become a venue that houses reviews, along with its real-world application. If you don't have this kind of technology in your classroom, it is fine to work with paper, reproducible versions.

I read the review line-by-line while students marked the parts on their own copy they deemed well written.

> Beep! Beep! Vrrooom! It's a traffic jam and the little red car can't move. It's your job to get the little red car moving! I think Rush Hour Traffic Jam is the best puzzle game. It is like a maze, but much more fun because you can choose from different levels to keep you thinking. There are four levels of difficulty.
>
> The box has easy-to-follow directions and inside you will find 40 challenge cards with the solutions printed on the back, just in case! You'll need to set up the cars and buses in a pattern on the road grid. Then, your job is to move the vehicles one by one, until the red car can escape. Guess what! If you don't have someone to play with, you can play this game alone! One time, I was waiting for my brother to finish his homework and this game kept me busy for two hours!
>
> Rush Hour Traffic Jam won a national award from Mensa and is also a Parents' Choice recommended toy. I give it two big thumbs up.

After reading one review, pause to muse over what the author had done that could be done again. Then read another.

I paused to think aloud. "Hmm . . . what does this review writer do to let us know her opinion about this game? What special parts does she include in her review to convince us?" I left a moment for students to think independently, disregarding raised hands, for now. Then, I moved on to read a second review. "Let's put the review of Rush Hour to the side for just a moment and do the same work with this review of *The Incredibles*. My nephew loves movies, too, especially ones about superheroes. A new DVD would make a great birthday gift. Get your Post-it notes ready to mark parts that stand out and feel especially convincing.

> Do you like reading comic books? Do you love Batman or Spiderman or Wonder Woman? Do you ever wish you had super powers? If you do, then you need to go see <u>The Incredibles</u> right now! Everything you love about superheroes is in this movie!
>
> The movie is about a whole family of superheroes, except they act, and sort of look, like a normal family. Mr. Incredible used to be one of the toughest superheros, but now he works in a boring office. His wife, Helen, has also given up her superhero outfit and now she uses her special powers to be a mom. Their son, Dash, uses his super speed to be great at sports. Violet, who has the ability to turn invisible and enclose herself inside a force field, acts like any normal teenager. The baby, Jack . . . Jack doesn't seem to have any super powers at all, at least, not yet! The evil villain, Syndrome, starts up the action and the Incredibles are back in superhero mode in no time!
>
> You will love <u>The Incredibles</u>. This movie is nonstop fun! Last time I watched this movie, I laughed so hard, my belly hurt. I recommend this movie for superhero fans of all ages. I give it 5 stars!

"These writers sure did a lot to make their reviews really convincing and get us to want to buy and play with these products!" Then, I prompted, "But now, I'd like you to discuss a huge question: What makes these reviews so convincing? Look closely. Read those parts again and think, 'What did this review writer do to get me thinking? What important parts did the writer make sure to include?' Do that quietly by yourself."

As I read, there were several spots where children signaled that the review seemed especially well written.

Readers, you'll want to think about what you notice these reviews have done. In this review, for example, the writer says the whole family has superpowers—a generalization—and then proceeds to methodically discuss each family member, one at a time. The writing is clear and structured.

Remember to gesture back to the question heading on your chart. Emphasize the "what important parts" so that children understand they are searching for multiple strategies inside the review.

Coach into children's work, prompting them to study structure, voice, word choice, and craft.

As children worked, I voiced over, "The answers are sometimes hard to find, so read the part once more and ask yourself: 'What is it about the part I like so much? Why did the writer decide to include these kinds of details?'"

I left a moment for students to do this inquiry work independently. Then, I signaled, "Writers, point to one thing that the review writer did to convince you." They did. Then I said, "Think about what *exactly* makes that part stand out. What can we name it?" I added, "Turn and share what you notice with your partner." I listened in as students spoke, taking note of important observations that I could highlight when the group came back together.

Reconvene the group, and restate the details students noticed to create a class list.

"Writers, I'm hearing you share so many smart things these two review writers did to convince readers. Let's make a big list of all of the things you noticed to help us keep track, so we can challenge ourselves to try this in our reviews, too. Who wants to start?"

"It tells you about it, like what it is. But not everything, just so you get an idea," Skylee began. "You're right, like a sneak peek to help understand the topic better," I rephrased. "And it tells you information about it. Like how the game got awards and stuff," Bradley tagged on. "Also, there was a little story in the first one. He said how he was waiting to play with his brother, and he played the puzzle by himself, instead," Tucker noted, holding up the game review.

As kids continued to share out their observations, I reworded them in clear and concise ways, as I recorded their ideas and added them to our anchor chart.

"Wow, such an impressive and challenging list! This will be very grown-up work for you to try, and I'm wondering who in our class might be ready to reach for the stars in their review writing today!" Arms stretched out toward the ceiling, taking on this challenge.

Send writers off to work independently.

"Review writers, it's time for us to get started. Remember, when you write reviews, you'll write using all that you already know about opinion writing—stating your opinion and making sure to supply reasons," I began, gesturing toward the main part of the chart outlining the expectations across the checklist. "But, maybe some of you will also try to do some of this very grown-up and challenging work that review writers in the world do when they write to convince readers," I urged, tapping across the stars surrounding the chart.

"Give me a thumbs up if you feel ready to go off and start writing lots and lots of reviews!" Most of the thumbs waved high in the air, so I nodded consent. "Great! Off you go. But, if you need a minute more to generate some ideas, stick here on the rug with me."

Allowing time for children to think, then share with a turn-and-talk partner before you ask them to create a list together offers children plenty of rehearsal time. As the children name their noticings, you may decide to say back what they are saying in clear, memorable phrases so that children understand you are giving these strategies a name.

You'll need to decide, in an instance such as this, whether the list you compile today becomes an anchor chart, which means it threads its way through many minilessons and travels across units. We think it's best to regard this as a quick jotting, and to reteach the key items on it more slowly, and only then to cumulate them on an anchor chart.

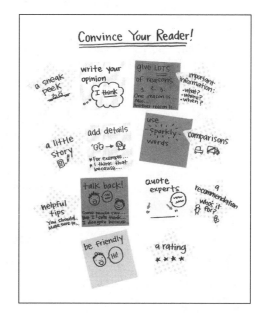

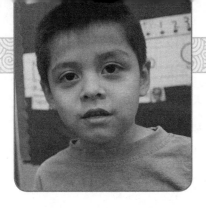

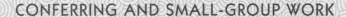
Highlighting the Work of Individual Students as a Way to Invite Others to Give It a Try

WHILE TODAY IS THE FIRST DAY OF REVIEW WRITING, it is not your students' first day of opinion writing. Expect that students are comfortable with forming and stating opinions, and be sure to tuck in plenty of compliment conferences today, taking time to point out the strong opinion strategies they are carrying into their work as reviewers.

You'll want to walk around with the Opinion Writing Checklist, Grade 1 and Grade 2 in hand as you confer with children, using it to pinpoint strengths and assess needs,

determining next steps you'll take across the coming days and weeks. For example, you might notice how a child makes sure to state his opinion right at the start, making it crystal clear to the reader. Meanwhile, you'll want to take notes to account for any strategies for elaboration, focus, or conventions that require further support, teaching that you'll address in your minilessons and future conferring work.

Instead of lingering with each child to tackle this teaching today, quickly move from student to student and from table to table, to deliver these compliment conferences at

MID-WORKSHOP TEACHING Rating Systems for Persuasive Reviews

"Writers," I said as I stood up from a table in the middle of the classroom, "eyes up on me! I want to share with you something so clever that Caleb thought up for his review that you might want to try in your own writing." I held up Caleb's writing for the rest of the class to see. "Caleb is working on a review about Angry Birds, the game." Immediately, supporters of the game piped up with enthusiasm. "Well, Caleb definitely loves the game, too. Right here," I said, pointing to a space at the top of his paper, "he drew *five* birds. Do you know why he did that?" I nodded toward Caleb to fill in his explanation.

"Because that means it's super fun. No birds would mean it's boring, but I gave it five angry birds to show that I really, really, really like it. I made it like that other

review with the stars. Except, I put angry birds instead of stars, because I love Angry Birds!" Caleb cheered.

Then, I invited the rest of the writers to do this work, restating this as a strategy all the children could try. "Reviewers often use a rating system to show how much they liked or didn't like something. If you loved something very much, you might decide to award it five whole stars, or if it was just so-so, maybe it will only get three stars. But if you thought, 'No way, nuh-uh, never ever, again! I can't stand it!' you might not give *any* stars, or just a half star, or one teeny tiny little star. You might use stars or something else you think up, like Caleb did. But, whatever system you decide to use, you'll want to make sure you write your opinion and reasons to explain why you gave it that rating."

As Students Continue Working . . .

"Writers," I said as I stepped to the middle of the classroom, "pens down, eyes up." After I had every child's attention, I began, "I see that many of you are writing reviews about things or places you've tried and absolutely *loved*. This is important work. It's helpful to think about things that *you* really enjoy to write reviews that convince others to try them, too! Let me remind you that sometimes reviewers choose to write about things or places that are not so great, maybe even totally terrible! That way, they can warn people to stay away! Those topics are important to write about, too."

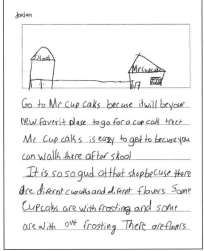

Jordan

Go to Mr cup caks becuse it will be your
new faverit plase to go for a cup cak treet
Mr Cup calks is eazy to get to becuse you
can walk there after skool
    It is so so gud at that shop becuse there
are difernt cupcaks and difrnt flavers Some
cupcaks are with frosting and some
are with out frosting There are flavers

like PB n J that meens penut butter and
jelly cupcak with straw barry frosting
And there are flavers like snoball
witch is cokonut frosting and chocolat
cak cupcak

FIG. 8–1   Jordan supplied clear reasons to support his claim.

Opinion Writing Checklist

	Grade 1	NOT YET	STARTING TO	YES!	Grade 2	NOT YET	STARTING TO	YES!
	Structure				**Structure**			
Overall	I wrote my opinion or my likes and dislikes and said why.	☐	☐	☐	I wrote my opinion or my likes and dislikes and gave reasons for my opinion.	☐	☐	☐
Lead	I wrote a beginning in which I got readers' attention. I named the topic or text I was writing about and gave my opinion.	☐	☐	☐	I wrote a beginning in which I not only gave my opinion, but also set readers up to expect that my writing would try to convince them of it.	☐	☐	☐
Transitions	I said more about my opinion and used words such as *and* and *because*.	☐	☐	☐	I connected parts of my piece using words such as *also*, *another*, and *because*.	☐	☐	☐
Ending	I wrote an ending for my piece.	☐	☐	☐	I wrote an ending in which I reminded readers of my opinion.	☐	☐	☐
Organization	I wrote a part where I got readers' attention and a part where I said more.	☐	☐	☐	My piece had different parts; I wrote a lot of lines for each part.	☐	☐	☐
	Development				**Development**			
Elaboration	I wrote at least one reason for my opinion.	☐	☐	☐	I wrote at least two reasons and wrote at least a few sentences about each one.	☐	☐	☐
Craft	I used labels and words to give details.	☐	☐	☐	I chose words that would make readers agree with my opinion.	☐	☐	☐
	Language Conventions				**Language Conventions**			
Spelling	I used all I knew about words and chunks of words (*at*, *op*, *it*, etc.) to help me spell.	☐	☐	☐	To spell a word, I used what I knew about spelling patterns (*tion*, *er*, *ly*, etc.).	☐	☐	☐
	I spelled all the word wall words right and used the word wall to help me spell other words.	☐	☐	☐	I spelled all of the word wall words correctly and used the word wall to help me figure out how to spell other words.	☐	☐	☐

a pace that allows you to capture a clear and sweeping snapshot of the overarching strengths and needs of your classroom.

I stopped for a moment at Jordan's table, quietly observing the children as they wrote. I paused beside Jordan, as he worked on his review of a local bakery (see Figure 8–1). It was already quite clear that Jordan had begun with a clear opinion and remembered to supply many reasons to support his claim. I made sure to invite the other children at the table to practice this strategy, too.

> Go to Mr. Cupcakes because it will be your new favorite place to go for a cupcake treat. Mr. Cupcakes is easy to get to because you can walk there after school.
>
> It is so so good at that shop because there are different cupcakes and different flavors. Some cupcakes are with frosting and some are without frosting. There are flavors that are like PB&J that means peanut butter and jelly cupcake with strawberry frosting. And there are flavors like snowball which is coconut frosting and chocolate cake cupcake.

I stopped the table from their writing. "Red table, I can tell you are very hard at work. Put your pens down for just a moment." I waited until the children had paused from their writing and looked up at me, before continuing.

"I want to share with you something so smart that Jordan is remembering to do as he writes his review." Jordan smiled proudly, sitting up taller in his chair. I held up Jordan's paper and highlighted the strategy in a way that would make it transferable to the other students' work. "Jordan is reviewing Mr. Cupcakes, a bakery nearby," I explained.

"Oh! I know that place! It's so good there," Leander chimed in.

(continues)

"Well, Jordan agrees with you, and I know that because he remembered to begin his review by stating his opinion clearly, right from the very start," I said, pointing to the top line of the page.

"But that's not all. He didn't just stop there and expect people to agree. Oh no! Instead, he kept going to make his review extra convincing by giving *lots* of reasons and details. He used the word *because* to say why people should go to Mr. Cupcakes and even gave details about the kinds of cupcakes and flavors they have."

Then, I invited the rest of the table to take on the work Jordan's piece had demonstrated, prompting the others to transfer these skills into their review writing. "I bet you can all do that, too! I bet Jordan can find even more places to keep at it. Remember, if you want to write a review that really convinces your readers to agree with your opinion, it's important to make your opinion clear from the very start of your piece. Then, to make that opinion even stronger, you'll want to give lots of reasons and details and say, *because*, to tell why." I gestured for the students to return to their pieces. Before moving on to the next table, I recorded notes in my conference binder to jot the strengths I had observed in Jordan's writing, along with next steps to support elaboration—strategies that I would be sure to address in my future conferences, small-group work, and minilessons.

Using Tiny Topic Notepads to Collect Topic Ideas for Reviews

Generate a list of possible topics for review. Invite children to use tiny topic notepads to jot topic ideas.

To prepare for today's share, I placed a tiny topic notepad at each rug spot and asked children to come to the meeting area with their writing pens. I had noticed that many of my writers had drafted only a single review across today's session, and I wanted to increase volume right from the start of this second bend.

"Reviewers, let's make a plan for *tomorrow's* writing. Think about all the topics you could review. Think about the world outside our classroom and the places and things you know. What *else* might you write about so your readers will know to try it, or to stay away?" I gave the students a moment to think, signaling for eager participants to ponder further. "Let's make a chart together that we can use to help us find ideas for review after review after review! This way, we'll make sure to fill up our folders!"

"*Toy Story*! Mario Party!" piped Vada, naming actual examples in the room.

"Vada notices that we could write reviews on *things* we've experienced, like movies and games." As I said this, I turned to the chart and made the first bullet point with the word "Things" in big and bold letters, quickly writing "games" and "movies" on Post-it notes and adding it to the chart, helping students see the subcategories below the broader category. "Are those the only kinds of *things* reviewers might write about?"

"Batman toys!" Tori exclaimed. On a third Post-it note, I wrote, "toys" and added it as well, then turned back to face the writers. "Vacation places!" spouted Boone. "I go to Cape May every summer. It's the best!"

"*Places* like restaurants and vacation spots and cities that you've visited are certainly topics you could write reviews about, too!" I added, and turned back to add these to the chart.

"On your rug spot, there is a tiny topic notepad for you to use. Right now, jot some of the topics you already have in mind to plan for the reviews you'll write tomorrow!" I gave students a moment to quickly record these ideas.

"Carry these tiny topic notepads with you because now you are review writers, and to live like a review writer, you'll want to collect ideas *everywhere* you go—in the cafeteria, listening to the radio in the car, watching a television show."

Talking Right to Readers

IN THIS SESSION, you'll teach students that writers use a persuasive voice by writing as though they are talking right to their readers, offering important information.

GETTING READY

✔ "Important Information" chart (see Teaching)

✔ Your own review, enlarged and ready for revision (see Teaching)

✔ Student writing folders (see Active Engagement and Share)

✔ Index cards to write minilists on (see Conferring and Small-Group Work)

✔ "Convince Your Reader!" chart (see Share)

COMMON CORE STATE STANDARDS: W.1.1, W.1.5, RFS.1.4, SL.1.1, SL.1.4, L.1.1.d, L.1.2, L.1.6

HAVE YOU EVER FOUND YOURSELF humming a jingle from a fast-food restaurant or an insurance company? It's true that jingles attract attention and persist in our memories in ways we sometimes wish didn't happen. But, it is not the jingle itself that persuades us to go to the new restaurant in the neighborhood, nor is it the clever mascot, like that charming lizard that makes you think twice about your insurance rate. Instead, the true art of advertisement stems from the information offered within each commercial, relaying facts that impress, surprise, or intrigue. When you hear that a grocery store is open twenty-four hours or that it has a bank with an ATM right inside, you're apt to tuck that knowledge away and use it at the eleventh hour when you are icing your son's birthday cake and realize you don't have candles or a crisp five-dollar bill to tuck inside his birthday card.

The information and recommendations contained in commercials is what companies work hardest to craft, deciding what to include in those brief seconds of airtime. It is what review writers need to do as well. What is it that makes you decide to go ahead and purchase a movie ticket after reading a review? What helps you decide which vacation spot to visit over another? Most likely, it is the information provided by the reviewer.

We are not suggesting that you teach your writers to use exaggeration or tomfoolery to convince others, in fact, quite the opposite! While children are often quick to make grand claims, you'll teach writers to be careful not to make outlandish promises or deliver exaggerated descriptions, listing one fantastic, incredible, exciting, great, and terrific adjective after another. After all, those kinds of details make writing *less* convincing.

Today's session highlights the importance of writing reviews with a persuasive voice that speaks to readers, delivering relevant and pertinent information in a friendly, helpful, and well-informed tone to gain trust and to convince. You'll teach children to rehearse this voice aloud, imagining that their reader is standing right beside them, planning the words they'll include, much like an announcer in a commercial does when he speaks as though he knows exactly what you want and why you need it.

Expect that children will rush off to begin, eager to persuade their readers and write information into their reviews. But you'll want to remind students that as writers learn new strategies to make their pieces stronger, it's especially important to use these strategies to revise—returning to earlier drafts and finding opportunities to cement this work. Be sure to stock your writing center with plenty of revision materials, as well as have these tools on hand, while you meet with students during individual conferences and small groups.

> *"As writers learn new strategies to make their pieces stronger, it's especially important to use these strategies to revise."*

Of course, with this newfound sense of authority, it'll be important to remind writers of the fine line between convincing and being bossy. You'll ask your writers to reread often and to watch their tone, making sure to speak, and write, in a persuasive, yet friendly, tone rather than a demanding one.

By the end of today's session, it's quite possible that the volume of students' reviews will nearly double. Writers who began with no more than five lines of writing on a page may now have closer to ten. Once children realize the value of including important information in convincing readers, they'll bring all they know about informational writing into their persuasive work. Your share will help them to check, this time with a partner, that their voice continues to persuade, rather than demand, and that the information they've chosen to offer readers is information that helps convince, and not simply teach.

Talking Right to Readers

CONNECTION

Describe a time when a commercial persuaded you of something.

"Last night, just before bedtime, I was snuggled up on the couch watching television when I decided I wanted a little late-night snack. A commercial came on, and I heard a voice coming from the TV. The voice said, 'It's late, and I know what you *really want* is something cool and refreshing . . .' I felt like the voice was talking right to me! I watched as a picture of a milkshake came onto the screen, and then the voice said, 'We start with cool, creamy ice cream. Then we add fresh berries. We mix it together and serve it to you icy cold with whipped cream and a cherry . . .' I thought, 'Hey, a milkshake does sound really good right now!'

"Then the announcer said, 'You're not too far! We have convenient locations . . .' and then he told where those locations were.

"'Oh, good,' I thought, 'It's really close. I could even walk.' So right at that very moment I was *convinced*. I stood up from the couch and said to myself, 'I want a milkshake. I need a milkshake. I *must have a milkshake*!'"

Connect the persuasive tone of commercials to that of review writers.

I paused from my story to address the class. "You know, the way that announcer in the commercial was talking made it seem as if he were standing right in my living room talking to me. He knew all the information that I needed to hear to convince me to get up and try that milkshake—making sure to tell me about *what* it is, and *where* to find it. That information made the commercial even more convincing. That's just the kind of work you can do in your reviews. When you write reviews to convince readers, it's almost as if you're making a commercial on your topic, and it will be important to use that same kind of voice."

❖ **Name the teaching point.**

"Today I want to teach you that review writers include important information to convince their readers. One way to do this is to use a voice that talks right to your reader, explaining what your topic is, where to find it, and when to go."

Notice that this is really a Small Moment story. To write it, I used all the techniques that children learn. The story is focused. It begins by creating a scene and then showing what I'm doing at that place, in that moment. It includes direct dialogue. When you write minilessons, remember to use all you know about good writing to help you.

One scaffold you may decide to use during this connection is to have two sentence strips—one with the words, "What it is" and the other with, "Where to find it"—so that children can see as well as hear the types of information you are teaching them to include in their reviews.

It helps to pause after you write a bit of text and to see if what you've written contains the qualities it needs in order to be convincing. These are ways we already know to be convincing.

TEACHING

Reference the anchor chart, drawing attention to the strategy of adding important information.

It helps to pause after your write a bit of a text and to see if what you've written contains the qualities it needs in order to be convincing. These are ways we already know to be convincing.

Important Information

- What?
- Where?
- When?

Work together with writers to draft a piece of shared writing that shows a clear example of using a persuasive voice to inform.

"Watch how I try directly speaking to readers, giving them the information they need, in my review of Pinkberry," I began, turning to the easel where I had an oversized piece of review paper clipped to the board. I read what I'd already written aloud:

> Pinkberry is a good place to go for a treat. There are a lot of flavors and a lot of toppings.
> Pinkberry is fun to go to with a friend.

"Hmm . . ." I said, looking critically over my writing and reading it again under my breath. "Well, I'm definitely writing my opinion and giving reasons for my thinking, but my writing doesn't sound like the announcer of a commercial. I don't sound like I'm talking to my readers, and I'm not giving a whole lot of information that is convincing, either. I might need to revise this."

Turning from the easel, I proposed a planning strategy to aid this revision. "Let's imagine that there are readers standing right beside me. I can talk right to them to plan out loud the words I might add." Then, I thought aloud to myself, "Hmm . . . what should I say? What important information will they need to know? I'll need to make sure I use a friendly tone if I want to convince them to go to Pinkberry."

"Let's see, maybe I can start by saying something like, 'Did you know that frozen yogurt is just as delicious as ice cream, but it's actually good for you?' Or maybe I could say, 'If you love ice cream, then I know you'll love the frozen yogurt at Pinkberry! It is super healthy and delicious.' Or maybe I could start by saying, 'I've had a lot of frozen treats, but the best frozen treat I've ever had is the yogurt at Pinkberry!'"

Teachers, this minilesson has a double-decker teaching point, which can actually be a bit confusing to kids and to you as well. This minilesson is about the power of directly addressing readers and about the importance of answering essential questions in a review. If this combination seems a bit awkward, you are right!

By purposefully struggling, pondering a bit before proceeding, I show students how important it is to rehearse several possibilities, rather than just coming up with one and committing it to paper immediately.

"Okay, so let me go back and reread the start of my review so I can revise it to sound more like I'm talking to my readers, including information that they will want to know." I reread the first sentence:

Pinkberry is a good place to go for a treat.

"No, that's not quite like how I talk." I drew a line through the sentence and tried a new sentence:

If you love ice cream, then I know you'll love the frozen yogurt at Pinkberry! It is super healthy and delicious.

"Now," I said, sitting back to admire my work, "*that* sounds like I am talking right to my readers, and it has important information about *what* Pinkberry is. Let me reread the next part:"

Pinkberry is fun to go to with a friend.

Then, I paused to plan for further revision. "Well, I know it'll be helpful to teach readers *where* they can find Pinkberry, or even when to go. When I talk to my readers, I'll want to be sure to include this information." I turned my body toward my imaginary audience and rehearsed possibilities, "'You should bring your friends when you go to Pinkberry. There are always plenty of tables and chairs so you can sit down while you enjoy your dessert.' Or maybe, 'Pinkberry is a popular place to get frozen yogurt. There are flavors for everyone.'

"I can also add information about *when* to go." Then, turning back to my "readers," I voiced over, "'Did you know that Pinkberry is open all day long? You can go anytime you want a frozen treat!' Let me add this to include the kind of voice that talks to readers and teaches important information about the topic." I quickly added:

Pinkberry is a popular place to get frozen yogurt. You can find a Pinkberry in almost every neighborhood from here to Peru! There is probably one close to you, too. Did you know that Pinkberry is open all day long? You can go anytime you want a frozen treat!

Restate your process in a way that makes the strategy transferable.

"Did you notice how I planned by imagining that readers were standing right here beside me and said out loud the words I could add to this review? I made sure to use a talking voice and to teach readers important information they'll need to know to convince them to try it, too, including what it is, where to find it, and when to go."

Originally, we'd written this teaching session so that it contained even more exchanges between the writer and an imaginary audience, but the point was made after just a bit of them. Youngsters won't glean subtleties from a demonstration such as this, so be content to make the main point.

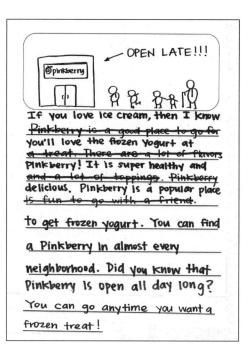

Notice that often, I restate the teaching point. I want to drive it home.

ACTIVE ENGAGEMENT

Give students an opportunity to orally rehearse talking directly to their readers in a convincing manner.

"Let's try some of this work together, right here and right now! Take out one of the reviews you've been working on, and reread it softly to yourself. Give me a thumbs up after you've reread."

I waited a few moments as the children reread, before continuing. "Okay, now imagine that you are sitting right beside your readers. If you were going to tell your readers about this topic, what would you say to them, and *how* would it sound? Remember to use a talking voice and to include the important information readers need." Again, I gestured toward the chart.

I moved in to briefly work with students, as they rehearsed independently, reminding them to speak in direct address to their audience, and coaching them to add relevant information about their topic.

"Now, turn and tell your partner what else you might say in your review to give your readers important information about your topic." I prompted partners to rehearse together, speaking aloud the words they might soon write.

LINK

Send students off, reminding them of the options they have for their independent writing.

"Writers, as you go off to work today, I have a feeling that I'll see you doing a few different things. Some of you will be revising the reviews you've already written, going back to make sure your writing sounds like talking. Many of you will probably start new reviews, too. Whenever you start a new review, before you begin writing, stop and imagine that your readers are sitting right beside you. Then, think about what you would say if you were talking right to them. What would you say to convince them, and *how* would it sound? Write exactly those words on your page, making sure to include important information, such as what you are reviewing, where to find it, and when to go. This way, your reviews will have the kind of persuasive voice that really gets readers to listen."

Providing Follow-Up Conferences

Y ESTERDAY YOU ASSESSED your students' progress across the learning progression of opinion writing.

Today, I returned to Jordan. I'd worked with him earlier and wanted to follow up.

"Jordan, I see that you went back to your review of Mr. Cupcakes! What's your plan?"

"I think I'm going to add more about the kinds of cupcakes they have there," Jordan replied.

"You are very good at giving your reader lots of reasons you like the place and details! That's one way review writers work to convince their readers. Do you have other ideas about what to add?"

"About what to add?" Jordan skimmed his page and shook his head.

I added, "You can think to yourself, 'Once I've convinced readers to like the sound of this store, what information will they need to know?' Your review can almost be a bit like an information book, telling the facts that matter."

"Like where to find it, and when you can go!" Jordan interrupted, filling in, as he pointed up toward the chart.

"You got it! I bet if you included information like that in your reviews, people would have the kinds of details they'll need."

"I know! I could put that it's right near School #2, so that way people know which school it's by," Jordan decided. He began writing on a fresh, new page (see Figure 9–1).

> Mr. Cupcake is right near School #2 so you can walk there after school with your mom or baby sitter.

MID-WORKSHOP TEACHING
Talking Back to Your Readers Who Disagree

"Review writers, can I stop you a moment?" I asked, as I moved to the easel where the Pinkberry review I'd started earlier was still clipped. I want to remind you of another way to talk to your readers to make your writing even *more* convincing.

"Remember, you can talk *back* to people who might disagree. To do this, writers use phrases like, 'Some people think . . . but . . .' or, 'Others might say . . . but . . .'"

I put the two phrases on the board and touched the first one, "Watch me talk back to readers who might have a different opinion than mine of Pinkberry." I read my piece, then added out loud, writing my revisions in the air, "'Some people think Pinkberry is too expensive.'" Then I added, 'But it is worth it!' I could even add, 'Others might say that Pinkberry smells funny when you walk inside, but that is because they are using yogurt, and yogurt smells a little sour. But, don't worry, it tastes totally delicious!'

"Talking *back* to readers is another way to make your writing convincing and persuasive. Try it now. Think about something people who might disagree with your opinion would say about your topic. Now turn to your partner and talk back to prove your opinion. Start with one of the phrases I have here." I gestured to the two sentence starters, "Turn and talk back!"

Less than a minute or so later, I voiced over, "Now add some of that talking back to the review you're working on right now."

It is always open after school and it is only $0.50 for the "after school special" cupcake and they are little cupcakes so it is not bad for you because it is a little treat, not a giant sugar cupcake. It has carrots and other stuff in it but it is good. It is not disgusting. It is good.

Don't go to the other cupcake places. Don't go to the bagel places. Go to Mr. Cupcakes. There are t-shirts to buy that Mr. Cupcakes and have a Mr. Cupcakes on the front and on the back.

As Jordan elaborated on his topic, I took a blank index card to make a mini-chart for Jordan to keep in his writing folder, reminding him to carry this strategy across the remainder of his piece and across all of his future reviews. On it, I jotted a miniature version of the chart, with questions such as, 'What is it?' and 'Where to find it.'

"So Jordan, remember to not just include reasons and details about your topic in your review but also the important information." Then, with the mini-chart in hand, I listed, "You can teach 1) what it is, 2) where to find it, and 3) when to go."

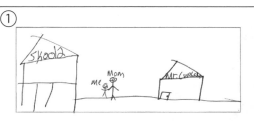

① Mr cupcah is right near skool 2 so you can walk there after skool (With your mom or baby siter Or if your brother is in 5 grade he can talke you too It is all ways open after skool and it is only 50 sents for the after skool speshal cupcah and they are littul cupcahs so it is not bad for you becuz it is a littul

② treet not a giant suger cupcah It has carets and uther stuff in it but it is good It is not desgusteng It is good Dont go to the other cupcah plases Dont go to the bagel plases Go to Mr Cupcaks there are t shirt to buy that say Mr cupcaks and have a Mr Cupcaks on the front and on the bak.

FIG. 9–1 Jordan's review aims to give readers the information they need.

Tone
Persuasive Not Bossy

Give students an opportunity to read their writing with their partners, making sure that their tone is persuasive and not bossy.

"Writers, sometimes, when writers write to persuade, it can start to sound a little bossy, and persuasive writers *never* want to sound bossy. Instead, they want to sound smart and helpful and friendly. The best way to make sure your writing isn't getting too bossy is to read it to your partner and do a check to make sure your writing is friendly.

"Right now, get close with your writing partner and work together to make sure your reviews are convincing, not demanding. Partner 1, you read first. Partner 2, listen closely to notice parts that might sound a little bit bossy. If you notice a part like that, stop and think about a better way to talk to your reader. You can ask, 'How else can I say this to convince my readers in a friendly way?' Then, you can revise to fix up those parts to make sure your reviews convince readers, rather than scare them away." I added this strategy to the chart.

Making Comparisons in Writing

R AY BRADBURY ONCE SAID, "Quantity produces quality. If you only write a few things, you're doomed" (*Writer's Digest* interview February 1976). We hope you'll carry these words with you as you hold expectations high, encouraging your writers to produce review after review, so that in just a few days' time, a healthy stack of reviews will fill each folder. Today's session suggests teaching writers to take all they know about opinion writing and lift the level of their work across all the reviews in their folders.

In today's session, you make students aware that when the quality of their work is uneven, this can be an invitation to roll up their sleeves. You'll probably use your mid-workshop voiceovers to exclaim and challenge writers to look again at reviews on the "done" side of their folders and ask themselves some serious questions: "Are these reviews *truly* done?" "Have I done all that I can to each and every one of my reviews?" Kids will be quick to admit, "No, I haven't revised *every* review in my folder," and with your encouragement, they'll move drafts from the "done" side of their folders to the "still working" side.

The teaching you'll do during today's minilesson will also add to students' growing repertoire, reminding them that they can use comparisons in their review writing, much as they did when ranking items in their collections. It's important that students are given opportunities to transfer strategies they've already learned into new work, exploring ways to apply these skills from various angles.

In this session, specifically, you'll help your children connect the writing they did at the start of this unit with the review writing they're doing now. Earlier, they studied their collections, studying individual attributes to select their "Best in Show" choice. Now, you'll teach writers to consider the attributes of their subject, comparing their restaurant or their movie or their game to those in other restaurants, movies, or games. These comparisons add credibility to claims students make.

IN THIS SESSION, you'll teach students that persuasive writers make comparisons. They include ways that their topic is better (or worse) than others.

GETTING READY

✔ A copy of student writing from the first bend of the unit (see Connection)

✔ Your own unrevised review from the previous session (see Teaching)

✔ Student writing folders (see Active Engagement)

✔ "Check Out This Review!" chart (see Mid-Workshop Teaching)

COMMON CORE STATE STANDARDS: W.1.1, W.1.3, W.1.5, W.2.1, RFS.1.4, SL.1.1, L.1.1, L.1.2, L.1.6

Making Comparisons in Writing

CONNECTION

Tell a story of a student who wrote using comparisons during the first bend of the unit.

I called students to the meeting area with their writing folders. Once everyone had settled into their spots, tucking their folders beneath them, I began, "Writers, when you began opinion writing, the first thing you did was line up each item of your collection in a row; then you looked at each very carefully, comparing an attribute from one item to the next, and deciding which was your favorite. When Roselyn wrote about her favorite Tech Deck skateboard toy, she lined up each and every one of her skateboards, and first she looked closely at all the wheels. She decided, 'The wheels on this Tech Deck are *better* than the wheels on this other Tech Deck because these are much smoother. Also, the wheels are yellow, and the other Tech Decks have plain black wheels.' The way Roselyn compared the wheels of each Tech Deck and then wrote how the Plan B Tech Deck was better because the wheels are smoother and because they are yellow." Roselyn beamed proudly from her rug spot.

I continued, linking students' earlier work to the current pursuit of review writing. "The work you did when writing about your collections is the work you'll need to bring with you as you write reviews. Taking one attribute or one subtopic—like wheels—and looking at that across many competing things (in this case, skateboards) is one way that review writers make their reviews more persuasive. They think about what makes their topics better (or, if you are writing a review telling people to stay away, what makes it worse) than others. They make comparisons."

❖ Name the teaching point.

"Today I want to remind you to use all you already know about writing to convince others. You can think about a way that your subject is better (or worse) than others. You compare your subject with others, thinking only about that one way, that attribute. Then, you can write to include this information in your review."

TEACHING

Model revising your own writing by coming up with comparisons.

"Watch how I do this in the review of Pinkberry. First, I'll need to reread and think about how to compare it to others.

◆ COACHING

Naming what the children did previously when they wrote about their collections—in this case, writing comparisons—serves as a scaffold for the work of today. It's important to remember that while you expect a higher level of comparison writing this time around, many of your children have experience with comparisons, and you'll want to call on that knowledge as you set forth today's teaching.

Some people think Pinkberry is too expensive, but it is worth it! Others might say that Pinkberry smells funny when you walk inside, but that is because they are using yogurt and yogurt smells a little sour. But don't worry, it tastes totally delicious!

The yogurt at Pinkberry is better than ice cream because it isn't as sugary. Ice cream tastes too sweet and Pinkberry is tart and fruity.

"Okay," I sighed, glancing toward the writers on the rug. "I bet I can make a comparison that suggests Pinkberry is better than other ice cream places. I'm not sure how to start. Hmmm. . . ."

Paula rocked forward and offered, "You should figure out what you want to compare. Like, you could compare the flavors they have or the toppings they have."

After just a moment, Boone's hand crept into the air. I nodded. "You could tell about how it tastes better."

"Both of you are absolutely right! That is the first thing we need to do when making a comparison. We can't just say it's better because, because, because. I need to think about *one way* to compare Pinkberry to other treat shops. I think I'll take Boone's advice and compare the *taste* of Pinkberry frozen yogurt to other ice creams. I could compare it by writing, 'The yogurt at Pinkberry is better than ice cream because it isn't as sugary. Ice cream tastes too sweet, and Pinkberry is tart and fruity.'" I leaned forward and revised my writing.

"Next, I could give more reasons why Pinkberry yogurt tastes better than ice cream. Or, I could make a different comparison—maybe writing about how Pinkberry offers better toppings than other ice cream shops. Either way, I'd be picking a subtopic—the taste, the topping—and comparing them at Pinkberry and at other places."

Notice that I call on just a very few children. The goal is to keep the minilesson moving along quickly so children have time to write.

ACTIVE ENGAGEMENT

Give students an opportunity to come up with comparisons for their own persuasive reviews.

"Review writers, take one of the reviews you've written, and try this work right now. Reread what you've written, and then think of a way to compare your topic to another. Give me a thumbs up when you've done a little rereading and thinking."

A few moments passed, and then I moved to the second part of the active engagement. "Okay, now, turn and tell your partner what you would write to make your writing more persuasive by making a comparison. Explain how it is better (or worse) than a competitor. Partner 1, will you start today?"

LINK

Send students off, reminding them of the various tools and options they have available today.

After partners shared their revision plans, I added, "Some of you may need to use revision strips because you may not have enough space where you'll want to add these comparisons. Revision strips show your readers how careful you are being when you take time to make your writing the best it can be."

Then, I moved on to restate the teaching point in a way to make it transferable to students' ongoing work as writers. "Remember, writers, whenever you are writing to convince people to agree with your opinion, persuading them to follow the recommendations you make in your reviews, it helps to not just claim that your subject is good (or bad), but also to claim that it is better or worse. To do that, think of a trait that you can compare—with my dog show, we compared eyes, fur, personality—and then look at the same trait in your subject, and in others. Compare.

I bet many of you will be busy working to strengthen your reviews today. And not only can you also make revisions to the reviews you are working on right now, but you can also make revisions to every review in your folder. This will make your writing stronger and more persuasive, and it will make *you* a stronger and more persuasive writer!"

Persuasive Writers Include Suggestions and Warnings

ONE OF THE BEST PARTS OF WORKSHOP TEACHING is the flexibility and responsiveness it offers us as teachers. Truly, what other methods of teaching allow you to move from the needs of the whole, to the needs of a group, to the needs of an individual and back again? Today, you might find yourself balancing the work of both small-group instruction and individualized conferring. Since the goal is for writers to work hard to revise across their reviews, you may find that your best course of action is to pull up to a table, admire a writer's work for just a moment, then stop the entire table and teach the others at the table to do the same work as that of the student you observed. For example, if you see a student dividing her attention between a classroom chart and her review, stop the table and call attention to the work that that writer is doing.

(continues)

MID-WORKSHOP TEACHING   Adding Supporting Details to Make Your Writing More Convincing

During today's mid-workshop teaching, I chose to spotlight the work that one child had done, adding supporting details to his persuasive writing. I had copied his original review onto chart paper so that everyone in the class could see.

"Writers, please put your pens down, and your eyes on Alejandro," I said, and gestured toward the front of the room, where Alejandro was standing holding his revised review. I walked over to stand beside him and said, "Alejandro is working hard to make his review as persuasive as he can by writing comparisons. I want to share his writing with you. Take a look at what Alejandro's review originally said." I pointed to the chart paper and read aloud.

> The Pirates is a great movie because of the adventure. The Captain is really funny and he makes a lot of mistakes but not on purpose. He is not a bad pirate but he acts like he is a tough guy.

"But, today I notice that Alejandro revised his writing to include more supporting details to back up his claim that the Captain acted like a tough guy. Listen for the new additions as Alejandro reads you his revised review."

> The Pirates is a great movie because of the adventure. The Captain is really funny and he makes a lot of mistakes but not on purpose. He is not a bad pirate but he acts like he is a tough guy. One way he tries to be tough is he tries to defeat Bellamy the other pirate in a pirate duel but they never have a real duel. Bellamy thinks he is a tough guy, too, but he is not tough. He is funny too but not as funny as the Captain.

"You can try that in your reviews, too. You can reread your reviews to find places where you can say even more to prove your thinking, adding more details that support your reasons. This will make your reviews even more persuasive."

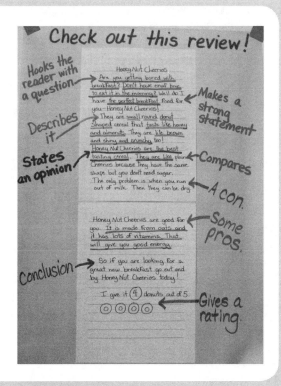

These table conferences help you keep one finger on the pulse of your classroom, as you move quickly from table to table, assessing skills and strategies. You may choose to gather three or four children who demonstrate a similar need, convening a small group in the meeting area.

I recently said to one such group, "I've been noticing that each of you has been working hard to make your reviews convincing, including lots of reasons and details. I want to teach you that review writers also give suggestions or warnings to help their readers. You can also add helpful advice.

"If I were to include a suggestion in this review of Pinkberry, I might add, 'You should get a Pinkberry loyalty card to earn a free cup of frozen yogurt!' Or, I might even add a warning, like, 'Pinkberry can get very busy after school is dismissed, so make sure to get there before 3:00 to avoid the crowds!'"

I made sure to keep my demonstration short, turning the work over to the students as quickly as possible. This way, I could devote the majority of the time to supporting each child with this strategy in their own writing. "Now, take out one of the pieces you've been working to revise, and think about how you might give suggestions or warnings to help your readers. What advice might you give?"

I gestured for the group to get started and I coached in with lean prompts to get each writer thinking. "Is there something I should watch out for?" "Should I bring something with me if I go there?" Once the students had begun to write, I pulled in to work with a writer who seemed to require some additional support.

"So, Amelia, this review is about Dolly's, one of our local restaurants. It looks like it's a 'stay away' review. You want to make sure people don't go there, huh?" I began.

"Yeah, it's so yucky!" Amelia remarked, sticking her tongue out in disgust.

"Wow, it seems you have a very clear opinion about that! Well, then, is there a warning that you might give about Dolly's?" I prompted.

Amelia looked up, tapping her chin in thought. "If they eat the fries, they should make sure to drink a lot, a lot, a lot of water because it is soooo salty."

"That's a big warning that you can write in your review. Decide where you'll add that tip into your writing." I gave Amelia time to reread and decide on this revision, moving on to check in with another writer. In a few moments, I glanced back at Amelia, who had finished recording her warning (see Figure 10–1).

I reconvened the group to celebrate their revisions and restate the teaching point in a way that encouraged the children to carry this work into all their work as review writers, sending them off to continue this practice across their whole folder.

Amelia's Review

Do not go to Dolly's because you will be sorry.

It is not good because it is salty.

It is not good because it does not have good food.

It is not good because it is dirty.

The french fries at Dolly's have too much salt on them and they stick in your throat.

You will need to drink a hundred drinks of water to get the taste out of your mouth.

Reason 2: The food is yuck!!!!!!! Yuck!

The salad bar was too messy and there was stuff in the wrong spots.

The carrot bowl had pieces of onions in it! GROSS!

If you try to get a carrot you got onion instead.

Someone clean it up! Put those carrots back!

Someone should clean it up.

It was dirty on the salad bar and on the floor and on the table.

It was dirty everywhere!

My mom said, "Let's leave. This is nasty" so we left and did not take our food!

FIG. 10–1   Amelia's review includes warnings to help readers.

Adding Small Moment Stories as a Means of Persuasion

Explain to writers that including Small Moment stories in their persuasive reviews can make their writing even more convincing.

"Writers, today you have done all kinds of remembering, using strategies you already know to find ways to make your reviews even better. Writers do this all the time. Whenever you write, it's important to make sure you carry along a whole suitcase of smart skills and strategies. That way, you'll be prepared for *any* journey you go on as a writer, ready to make *all* your writing the very best it can be." I spoke with exaggerated gestures, as if physically carrying an armload of baggage.

"I know that one kind of writing you have become very smart at in first grade is Small Moment writing. Did you know that review writers can use the smart strategies they know for writing *stories* to convince people when writing *reviews*? Many of you noticed this in the review we read closely together." I gestured toward the anchor chart.

"You can tell a little story about a time you went to, or played with, or tried what you are reviewing. You can tuck in a Small Moment story and tell it in your review. You can imagine exactly what happened and tell it bit by bit, explaining what made your topic so great, or so terrible! These Small Moments make your reasons even stronger and more convincing. By sharing your own experiences, you can help convince your readers."

Give students an opportunity to reread one of their reviews and think of a Small Moment story that could be added to it.

"Right now, reread one of the reviews you have been working hard to revise. Let's keep going to revise even more! As you reread your writing, think about a moment when you went to that place, or saw that movie or show, or played with that toy."

As students reread quietly, I voiced over, "If you're writing a review to convince people to try it, too, think about a Small Moment story that shows what exactly made it so great. But, if you're writing a stay-away review, think about a Small Moment that explains why it's totally awful."

After a moment, I prompted students to turn and plan with partners, reminding students of a familiar strategy. "Zoom into the most important part, tell your story across your fingers, saying what happened first, next, last." I moved in to coach students as they planned their anecdotes aloud.

These books are written by different combinations of authors, so we are not as apt to maintain the same metaphor across the school year as you will be. Here, a repertoire of skills is a suitcase of skills. In another unit, it's a toolkit. The important thing, however, is that minilessons often start by reminding children of their growing repertoire of skills and strategies and they end, often, by sending writers off to draw on all of this.

It is important to allow writers opportunities to plan. Oral rehearsal supports focus and structure while developing students' writing fluency. You may coach in with prompts to support their oral storytelling, such as, "One time . . . ," "Then . . . ," "Finally . . . "

Hook Your Reader

Writing Catchy Introductions and Conclusions

IN THIS SESSION, you'll teach students that writers write introductions to grab their readers' attention right from the very start. One way to do this is to talk directly to readers.

GETTING READY

✔ "Say Hello with a Catchy Introduction!" chart (see Teaching and Active Engagement)

✔ An easel and your own writing, enlarged (see Teaching, Active Engagement, and Share)

✔ Clipboards, student writing, pens (see Share)

✔ Restocked revision flaps in writing center (see Mid-Workshop Teaching)

✔ "Don't Forget to Say Goodbye!" chart, added to the bottom of the "Say Hello with a Catchy Introduction!" chart (see Share)

COMMON CORE STATE STANDARDS: W.1.1, W.1.5, W.2.1, RL.1.4, SL.1.1, L.1.1, L.1.2

A CROSS THIS UNIT, you've taught your children to write in persuasive ways, using words to compel their audience, convincing them to try a new restaurant, visit a local playground, buy the latest video game, or see a new movie. Today, you'll channel your students to use their powers of persuasion to captivate their audience from the very start, writing introductions that urge readers to read on! You'll also teach students to write conclusions.

The Common Core State Standards don't emphasize introductions for first-graders but do expect them to compose opinion pieces that provide some sense of closure (CCSS W 1.1). Today, you'll teach your students to do this and more, working toward standards expected of second-grade writers. Of course, there are many ways to write introductions. Today's minilesson lays out one strategy writers can use to introduce their topic, providing a possible procedure for grabbing readers' attention from the start of a review. You'll collaborate with your students to compose a catchy introduction for a class piece, guiding writers to plan aloud to rehearse. It is likely that your students will recall this work from the work they did writing beginnings and endings to information books. You'll coach writers that one way to introduce a review is to start with a question, and you'll suggest that conclusions often restate the opinion and then send readers off to do something.

As you confer with writers, you may gather a group to study how a variety of reviews begin, closely reading each to discover different moves reviewers make. You may want to add to the chart you started during the minilesson, so that the class develops some alternate ways to write introductions. For example, you might begin with some of the same ideas students used to write Small Moments—sound words, action words, pop-out words, and so on. You can do a similar study of closings. A group can gather around some reviews to study how they conclude, developing a repertoire of methods for ending their reviews.

You may also decide to devote some of today's conferences and small groups to coach students to compose introductions. Remind writers to carry this work across their folders, working to write not just one introduction, but to revise introductions on all the reviews they will have written thus far in the unit. This will give them added practice.

Today's teaching share will shift writers' focus to conclusions. Just as you helped children understand how introductions are a way for writers to say, "Hi!" to their audience and to pull their readers in, conclusions are a way to say, "Bye!" and to send readers off. You'll teach students that conclusions leave the reader with a clear understanding of what the reviewer thinks about the topic. Children can do the same work with endings that they have done with their beginnings.

"Today, you'll channel your students to use their powers of persuasion to captivate their audience from the very start."

Hook Your Reader

Writing Catchy Introductions and Conclusions

CONNECTION

Tell the story of a time when a student in your class introduced himself to another student, and compare that interaction to the introductions writers make at the start of a review.

"I remember a month ago when Pete moved to our school all the way from Texas. Pete was sitting at his desk, and Gabe went over and said, 'My name is Gabe. Did you play math games on Fridays at your old school? We play math games every Friday. We love Snap the most of all. It's really fun. I'm good at Snap, and I could teach you to play if you don't know how. Do you want to play?'

Then, in a lackluster way, I impersonated the contrary. "You know, Gabe didn't just say, 'Do you know how to play Snap? I love to play it every Friday.'" I added, "No way! Gabe has better manners than that! Instead, he told Pete his name and asked him a friendly question. He *introduced* himself and told a little bit about our classroom and how it works.

"That same work that Gabe did when he *introduced* himself to Pete is what review writers do when they write reviews. Before they jump into their opinions and reasons, they introduce their topics. Introductions help grab readers' attention and get them to read on. There isn't just one way to do it, either. Writers write introductions in all sorts of ways. But today, I'm going to teach some ways you can write introductions to start your reviews."

❖ Name the teaching point.

"Today I want to teach you that writers write introductions to grab their readers' attention right from the very start. One way to do this is to talk to your reader."

Your children will love it if you mine the everyday moments of classroom life as sources for lessons about how to write. You won't, of course, tell this little story, but will instead substitute your own version of it. Keep your story brief, as the point is a simple one.

TEACHING AND ACTIVE ENGAGEMENT

Show students a chart you made that lists the steps to writing a catchy introduction.

"So, what kinds of things can you say to your readers in an introduction? How can you grab your readers' attention? One possible way to start a review is to ask questions to make your reader wonder. Then you can answer the question in a way that names the topic. Of course, your introduction also gives you time to say your opinion."

I tacked up the steps of the process to form a procedural chart to support independent practice of this strategy.

Teach through guided practice: take children through multiple cycles, channeling them to plan with a partner, write in the air while you coach, then elicit their work while you add comments.

"Let's return to the review of Pinkberry and work together to write a catchy introduction, one that will really grab people's attention and make them want to read on! Will you help me do that?" The class nodded as I clipped the enlarged demonstration piece to the easel. I reread the start of the review aloud to refamiliarize students with the text:

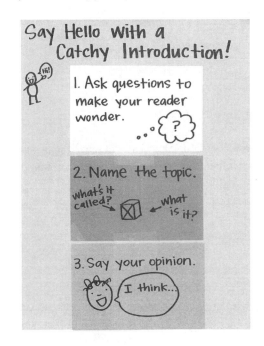

> If you love ice cream, then I know you'll love the frozen yogurt at Pinkberry! It is super healthy and delicious. Pinkberry is a popular place to get frozen yogurt. You can find a Pinkberry in almost every neighborhood from here to Peru! There is probably one close to you, too. Did you know that Pinkberry is open all day long? You can go anytime you want a frozen treat! Some people think Pinkberry is too expensive, but it is worth it!

Remind children of the strategy, and prompt students to plan possible introductions with a partner.

"So one way to grab people's attention is to start with questions that get readers wondering. You might say, 'Have you ever . . . ?' or 'Did you know . . . '" I offered, allowing my voice to trail off. "But you'll also want to name the topic so readers will know what the review is about."

For a minute, the room was quiet. "Thumbs up if you have ideas about what *you'd* say in an introduction about Pinkberry." I prompted partners to turn and plan together.

When we developed the opinion checklist and began reviewing on-demand opinion writing from hundreds of classrooms, it became clear that there were a few characteristics of CCSS opinion writing that we'd neglected to teach, and one was the introduction. Many of our students had grown accustomed to starting a piece by diving right in to the claim. We saw this trend throughout the grades. So this minilesson becomes an especially important one to us.

Naming three strategies in quick succession helps children to understand that while even one strategy (such as "Ask a Question") can introduce their topic, it isn't one tiny thing alone that makes a strong introduction, but several steps. This supports children with strategic thinking, so that you don't end up with twenty-five reviews all being introduced in the same ho-hum manner.

Coach with lean prompts that raise the level of what students do independently. Then convene the class to collect suggestions, writing in the air to compose an introduction collectively.

As the room erupted into talk, I moved across the meeting area to listen in and coach, as needed. "Pretend your partner is the reader. Use words that talk right to him." "Add your opinion to the end!" I nudged.

After a bit, I reconvened the class. "Let's come back together to collect our ideas and use all that we can to write the catchiest of catchy introductions! How shall we start it? What questions might we ask readers?"

"Did you know Pinkberry is the best place to get dessert?" Monique began.

"Did you know that it's good for you?" Tucker tagged on.

"Have you ever wanted something instead of ice cream for dessert?" Henry added.

"Wow, what compelling questions! Those are all great ways to begin our introduction." I echoed students' suggestions back. Then, turning back toward the students, I paused, as if to say, "Tell me! What is this review about?"

"Pinkberry!" the children all shouted.

"Remember to name the topic, and to state the claim," I instructed.

Soon we'd written this lead:

> Have you ever wanted something more exciting than ordinary ice cream for dessert? Did you know that frozen yogurt is delicious and actually good for you? Do you know the perfect place to go for fresh and tasty frozen yogurt?
>
> Pinkberry is a frozen yogurt shop that has all kinds of flavors and every topping you can imagine! You won't believe what you can put on top of frozen yogurt! I think Pinkberry is way better than any other ice cream place, even my cousin thinks it's awesome.

The interactive part of this teach offers children the opportunity to play and engage with language structure. Often children choose a sentence and stick with it, without thinking of other possible ways the writing could go. Engaging through play, and, even better, on your piece of writing, supports children in understanding that before we commit words to paper, writers often choose and rechoose sentences, letting the sound and flow of language dance across their tongues so that when they finally choose the words they want, it is with thoughtfulness and intent.

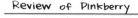

Review of Pinkberry

Have you ever wanted something more exciting than ordinary ice cream for dessert? Did you know that frozen yogurt is delicious and actually good for you? Do you know the perfect place to go for a fresh and tasty frozen yogurt?

Pinkberry is a frozen yogurt shop that has all kinds of flavors and every topping you can imagine! You won't believe what you can put on top of frozen yogurt! I think Pinkberry is way better than any other ice cream place, even my cousin thinks it's awesome.

LINK

Restate the teaching point in a way that makes this process transferable to students' independent work.

Today you've learned to write a catchy introduction that grabs people's attention. Remember that whenever you want to write an introduction, one possible way to do this is to ask a question, name your topic, and tell your opinion.

"I bet that many of you are itching to go off and get started on writing. You might want to look back at every review you've written so far and see if you can invent a great introduction. Today we studied just one way reviewers can make great introductions. I bet you could invent other ways as well!

"Of course, will you spend all day on introductions? No way! I'm pretty sure many of you will start new reviews today. Your Tiny Topics notepad can help you think of ideas."

Letting Student Intentions Guide Your Conferring

I SETTLED BESIDE MARCO, who had returned to a movie review that he had written earlier in the week. As he reread his piece out loud, I researched to ascertain Marco's strengths as a writer, as well as get a sense of his own intentions for the piece.

"Hey, Marco! How's it going?" I began.

"Good. I'm reading my review about the movie, *Chimpanzee*. It's really, really good. You should go see it!" he recommended.

"I bet that's why you decided to write a whole review about it—to convince people. What are you planning to do next with your review?" I inquired.

When Marco explained he wanted to make an introduction to make people want to see it, I echoed back what I heard. "So you plan to add an introduction to your review to grab your readers' attention and convince them to read your whole review and then go see the movie?"

"Yeah, but I can't give the whole thing away, because then the movie won't be as cool. Once my brother did that, and then it made the movie boring because I knew everything that was gonna happen."

"You're right. It'll be much more convincing to give a sneak peek, just like in a commercial, only telling a little bit," I added. Then, I continued with a compliment. "Marco, I must compliment you about something that impresses me so much. You're the kind of writer who really thinks about his writing and makes decisions about what to do next to make it even better. You could have just kept going with your review, or started a new piece, but instead, you went back to a piece that was already on the red-dot side of your folder and you reread it and found a way to make it better. That's a pretty grown-up thing to do," I praised.

I phrased my compliment in a way that highlighted a behavior that Marco may not have realized was important. By naming positive behaviors, you reinforce them. Then, I reminded Marco of what he'd learned about writing introductions. "So, now that you've decided to add an introduction to your review, you can use our class chart to help you plan it."

"I could say that if somebody says, 'Do you want to go see a movie?' you should say, 'Yes!'" Marco planned aloud. He reached for a revision flap to insert a new beginning:

> If someone says, "Do you want to go see a movie?" then you should say "Yes! Lets go see Chimpanzee!"

MID-WORKSHOP TEACHING   **Using Revision Tools**

I called for students to take a brief pause in their writing. Once all eyes were on me, I began. "Writers, I want to remind you to use revision tools to help you as you work today. Since introductions are meant to help readers get to know the topic and convince them to keep reading, it'll be important to add it to the very beginning of your review. You may need to use a revision flap to add your ideas," I explained, knowing this would be an important reminder for writers who set off to do this work independently today." So, I've restocked our writing center with plenty of flaps if you need to add space to the top of your piece. You might choose to write two introductions, trying out different ways it might go. Read it aloud to decide which version you like best, then tape it to the top of your review."

I pointed back toward the chart, reminding Marco of the second and third steps. "You'll want to tell a little bit about the movie and say your opinion."

"I think it's great!"

"Because . . ." I nudged.

"Because it has funny parts and sad parts. Oh, and also because it teaches you a lot about chimpanzees," Marco filled in. I tapped the next line of his paper, prompting him to add his ideas to his writing. He proceeded to write:

> It is a great movie because it has funny parts and sad parts. And it teaches a lot about chimpanzees and what they do.

"I like how you gave readers an idea about the movie without telling them everything that happens. That way, you can leave your readers wanting to know more. Is there something else you might want to say at the end of your introduction to get people to read on?"

"I can say that everyone will like this movie. It's not just a kids' movie," Marco said, quickly tagging on:

> Grown ups will like this movie and so will kids.

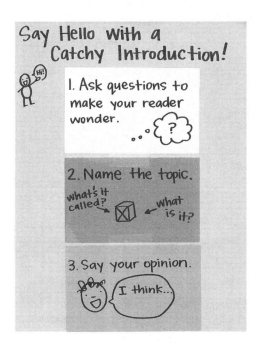

I asked Marco to read his introduction from the top (see Figure 11–1).

Marco's Review Revisions

If someone says, "Do you want to go see a movie?" you should say 'Yes! Let's go see Chimpanzee!' It is a great movie because it has funny parts and sad parts. And it teaches a lot about chimpanzees and what they do. Grown ups will like this movie and so will kids.

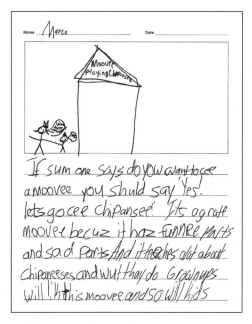

FIG. 11–1 Marco's review revisions

Then, I restated what he'd done, and encouraged him to revise all his reviews. "So, Marco, when you sat down to write this introduction, you began by asking a question to make your readers wonder. Then, you named your topic and told your readers your opinion about it. You can do this whenever you write an introduction to grab people's attention."

Crafting Catchy Conclusions

Explain the steps to writing a strong closing and model with your own writing.

I gathered the students back to the meeting area, asking that they each bring along a clipboard, their review, and a pen. Once the children had settled in their spots, I began, "Many of you spent today working on introductions to start your reviews. These introductions are a way for writers to say to readers, 'Hello! You should read this!' I want to teach you that writers also make sure to include a closing as a way to say, 'Bye! Thanks for reading!'

One way to write a conclusion is to restate your opinion, reminding readers of what you think or feel. Then, you can send your readers off to go do something! I unveiled a chart.

"If I were to add a closing to this review of Pinkberry, I'd want to make sure that readers remember exactly what I think. I might add a closing to say:

> I think Pinkberry is the best place for dessert because the frozen yogurt is tasty, healthy, and there are so many great toppings to put on top. Next time you are in the mood for a delicious treat, make sure you go to Pinkberry!

"So right now, take out the review you've been working on and think about how your closing might go. Whisper your closing into your hand to make a plan," I prompted, as students began composing, softly.

"Be sure to suggest what you think readers should go do," I voiced over.

After a few moments, I gathered the attention of the class. "Before you write those words down on your paper, turn and tell your partner how your closing might sound. Practice the words aloud together." I gestured for students to turn and share, rehearsing their closings before recording them.

"Now, quickly add your closing to the end of your review. And whenever you are writing to convince others, it is important to end with a closing. This way, your reader will be sure to remember your opinion and follow your recommendation."

Providing a sense of closure is one of the major standards held for first-grade writers, according to the Common Core. You may decide to remind writers of the work they did to include introductions and conclusions in their nonfiction books to help students transfer those skills to opinion writing.

You may choose to compose this conclusion aloud, writing in the air, and later add it to your demonstration piece as a means of keeping your teaching brief and allowing students more time to plan and draft their own conclusions.

I think Pinkberry is the best place for dessert because the frozen yogurt is tasty, healthy and there are so many great toppings to put on top. Next time you are in the mood for a delicious treat, make sure you go to Pinkberry!

Partners Work Together to Give Writing Checkups!

TOMORROW MARKS THE END OF THE SECOND BEND, and in preparation for the celebration that lies ahead, you'll want to remind writers to consider their audience, reviewing their pieces to check that they are clear and easy to read. Across this session, you'll ask writing partnerships to work together in ways that support editing.

The Common Core Language Standards expect first-graders to use upper- and lower-case letters (CCSS L 1.1), capitalize dates and names of people, use end punctuation, use commas in dates and lists, and use conventional spelling for words with common spelling patterns or high-frequency words (CCSS L 1.2). Today, you'll urge writers to make sure their reviews are easy to read, reminding them to check for spacing between words and capital letters. You'll also remind children to reflect on end punctuation.

Together, partners will read their pieces aloud, giving one another a "writing checkup" and providing suggestions to address ways to make each review more readable. You'll remind writers to check that they've used varied punctuation, cueing readers to stop, to use an asking voice, or to read words loudly. You'll also coach partners to use classroom resources to spell tricky words the best they can, using known words and word parts to spell.

The partnership work you facilitate across today's session directly supports the Speaking and Listening standards, which not only ask first-graders to participate in collaborative conversations (CCSS SL 1.1) but also expect students to ask and answer questions to gather information and clarify something that is not understood (CCSS SL 1.3).

You'll want to model this work with your own demonstration piece or with a shared class piece. You might want to fabricate a page of writing that contains many of the mistakes you often find in your children's pieces. As you collaboratively edit the demonstration piece during today's minilesson, you'll help children know how to make parts much clearer, to edit for punctuation, to capitalize, and to spell. You'll show writers that an important part of this process is to be thorough, moving down the page and across the piece, checking that each and every part is the best it can be—teaching your young writers to slow down, rather than hastily marking off their editing checklist.

IN THIS SESSION, you'll teach students that writing partners can read each other's writing and use an editing checklist to give feedback on how to make their writing better.

GETTING READY

✔ Student copies of "How Did I Make My Writing Easy to Read?" attached to clipboards, plus extra copies set out at tables, and enlarged version on chart paper (see Connection, Teaching, and Active Engagement)

✔ Enlarged copy of your own writing, in need of edits (see Teaching and Active Engagement)

✔ Student writing folders, editing pens (see Share)

COMMON CORE STATE STANDARDS: W.1.1, W.1.5, RFS.1.1, RFS.1.2, RFS.1.3, RFS.1.4, SL.1.1, SL.1.2, L.1.1, L.1.2

Certainly, you'll have writers who are making steady progress toward grade-level standards, while other students may need much more teacher support. You'll want to teach students within their zone of proximal development, rather than pushing students to adopt a practice that is well above the skill work they're ready for. Decide to use this conferring time to meet with students individually or in small groups to target specific needs. For example, perhaps you've noticed children who include proper punctuation, yet do so inconsistently. These are signals that students are ready for more explicit instruction, guiding them to listen for changes in their voice as they read aloud to cue them to add a period, an exclamation point, or a question mark as they write.

"An important part of this process is to be thorough, moving down the page and across the piece, checking that each and every part is the best it can be—teaching your young writers to slow down, rather than hastily marking off their editing checklist."

The work you'll rally writers to tackle today will undoubtedly support the writing they do across the next bend, as well as across their lives as writers, helping them to write in ways that are more readable from the very start!

Partners Work Together to Give Writing Checkups!

CONNECTION

Tell a story about going to the doctor's office for a thorough checkup.

When the children arrived on the rug, I had a clipboard with the familiar "How Did I Make My Writing Easy to Read?" editing checklist resting on my lap, a revision pen tucked behind my ear, and an air of seriousness about me. I had also placed a clipboard with a copy of the editing checklist on each student's rug spot. Once everyone settled, I began, "Last week I went to the doctor for a checkup. I was expecting a very quick visit, but that was definitely *not* the case!

"As soon as Dr. Walters walked into the room, she took out a clipboard with a long checklist. I sat on the table, and the doctor checked my heartbeat. She put the stethoscope over my heart and listened closely. Then, she took her checklist and made a little check in one of the boxes and wrote a little note beside her check mark."

Continue the story to help writers understand the importance of thoroughness.

"But she wasn't done yet! Next, she took a tiny, little light and looked inside both ears. She asked me if my ears felt itchy, and I told her that my ears felt fine. So, she took her checklist again and made a second little check mark on my list, and she wrote a few notes down on the paper. She made me open my mouth wide and say 'Ahhh . . .' while she examined my tonsils and my tongue. After that, she took a soft little hammer, and she tapped each of my knees with it!

"Do you know what she did after all that? You guessed it—she picked up her clipboard, made another check mark on her list, and wrote a bunch of notes on the paper."

Connect the doctor's thorough checkup to that of a writing partner.

"She was working really hard to check for *everything* to make sure I was okay. She didn't just check for one little thing to give me a checkup, she checked for *lots* of different things to make sure I was healthy.

"The same kind of work my doctor did to give me a checkup is one way you can work as a writing partner to help make sure your partner's work is the best it can be. You can be doctors of writing, giving your partner's piece a thorough checkup and leaving notes to help your partner's writing be as healthy as it can be."

◆ COACHING

The image of a doctor, doing a check up, conveys the air of responsibility and seriousness that we want to bring to this session. The doctor is careful, methodical, responsible—and that's what we hope writers will be as well.

During the last unit, you celebrated checklists by telling the story of the pilot— Captain Sullenberger—who landed a plane on the Hudson River by following a checklist. This is another try at elevating checklists!

❖ **Name the teaching point.**

"Today I want to teach you that writing partners can work together to give writing checkups. You can use an editing checklist to make sure your partner's piece is easy to read. If you see something to fix up, you can write a note, like a prescription, to give your partner ways to make his or her work even better."

TEACHING

Recruit children to join you in using the editing checklist to give your persuasive review a checkup.

"Will you all be my writing doctor and give this review a checkup?" I said as I posted the oversized copy of my review on the easel. The children quickly agreed. I gestured toward the "How Did I Make My Writing Easy to Read?" checklist I had displayed.

If you are able to do so, give youngsters a copy of your writing—enlarged so there is space for their edits. This way they'll be able to be more active during the minilesson. ❖

How Did I Make My Writing Easy to Read?

- I put spaces between my words.
- I checked the word wall.
- I spelled tricky words the best I can.
- I reread my writing, touching each word.
- I used capital letters at the beginning of sentences.
- I used different types of end punctuation.

"Let's start by looking at the first box on our checklist! The first item to check for is spaces between words. Doctors, ready? Let's check it!"

Page 1
wouLd you lik to laugH so hard that you shoot soda out of you Nose

Page 2
If you would then you should watch the movie call mega mind. becse it is the funniest movie you will ever see and you will love it a lot

Page 3
mega mind is a villain who wants to take over the city but instead he finds out he is really not a Bad guy at all

I had planted purposeful errors across the review, including misspelled words and run-on sentences, as well as numerous capitalization and punctuation errors. In doing so, I created an opportunity for close, critical reading and editing practice. My first page was free from spacing issues, but the beginning of my second page had some scrunched-together words. I did this purposefully to draw children's attention to reading on and thoroughly checking a piece. I saw evidence of this, as several revision pens hastily checked the first box.

"It looks like the first page has good spaces. But, remember to be thorough with your checkup! Let's check the next page!" I dramatically flipped my review to the second page where the words were squished together.

Some of the writers looked stunned, worried that they'd checked the box too soon. I gently reminded the class of the importance of taking your time, just like a doctor, checking every part to make sure it's the best it can be.

"Doctors, tell me what I need to do to make my writing better," I pleaded.

"You need to fix those squished-up words," Aiden said, as he pointed toward the piece. "Take a revision strip and write it with better spaces," he added.

"Okay, so when Aiden was giving my writing a thorough checkup for spacing, he gave me a prescription to put some spaces on the squished-up part," I echoed. "This will help me know how to make my piece better when I go back to edit."

"Now that we've finished checking for the first item on the checklist, let's go back and check for other ways to make this review easy to read. Go back to the checklist to look for more things to check for." I returned to the easel and began to reread aloud. I had only read a few sentences, when thumbs began waving feverishly in the air, with "doctors" anxious to check up my work.

"Whoa!" I paused from my reading, stunned that so many thumbs were already in the air. "Doctors, do you see something I should do to make my writing better before you can check the box on the checklist? Tell me, Dr. Rosa, what's your prescription? What can I do to make this piece better?" I asked.

"You need to start with an uppercase *W*! All sentences get uppercase letters at the beginning!" Rosa chimed.

"Oh!" I stammered, "I knew that! I must have forgotten to do that when I started this sentence."

"And you have uppercase *L* in that word. The rest have to be lowercase. Just the first one is big," Rosa continued.

"Oh my! I didn't even see that!" I muttered and quickly took a Post-it note to jot, "Check for capitals in wrong places!" Then, I attached it to my writing. "This will definitely help me make this review easier to read."

ACTIVE ENGAGEMENT

Give students a chance to continue to check over your writing in partnerships, using the editing checklist.

"Let's keep going. Right now, use your copy of the checklist to make notes about what I still need to do to fix up this review." I motioned for students to pick up their clipboards. "But this time, work together with your partner to talk about what you notice and what you would suggest I do to make my writing better." I prompted students to begin.

I settled beside a partnership and saw that Dalton had already ticked his box. Instead of intervening myself, I whispered to his partner, Sarah. "Sarah, remind Dalton to be thorough! Tell him to keep going and read all my pages," I prompted.

Sarah turned to Dalton and said, "Wait, Dalton. Keep going! You gotta read the second page, too. Don't just check it off."

"Oh yeah, I forgot," Dalton said and quickly scratched out his check mark, moving his eyes back to my review to read on, line by line.

"How smart of you both! You'll want to be very thorough, checking the whole piece and using your checklist to check for *lots* of different ways to make it better," I reminded before moving on to another set of partners.

LINK

Remind students of the importance of being thorough editors.

"So, writers, remember that whenever you are checking over your work, or your partner's work, it is important to take your time so you give one another a thorough checkup! Remember to reread the piece carefully, and if you find something to fix up, you can write it on a Post-it note to suggest ways to make it even better. In the middle of each table, I have left some new copies of the editing checklist to help you give each other writing checkups!" I sent the students off with partners to work.

When children are working with partners, as they often will be, resist the temptation to coach the writer directly, and instead whisper hints to the partner.

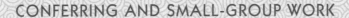

Teaching Capitalization via the Small-Group "Ripple Effect"

TODAY'S SMALL-GROUP WORK was actually planned yesterday when, during my prep, I'd gathered the writing folders from several tables and looked across pieces to assess students' understanding of capitalization. Since the start of first grade, the students and I had focused on uppercase and lowercase letters, with an emphasis on capitalizing beginnings of sentences.

All around the room was evidence of our focus, from the shared writing I'd done where each capital letter had been highlighted and celebrated together with the class, to our interactive writing pieces, which were plastered with Post-it notes showing how the writers had gone back to correct lowercase beginning sentences with uppercase beginnings, and to give place names a capital. (The words "Sunny Side Elementary School" had been a hot button topic. What, exactly, needed to be capitalized?)

When I looked across pieces inside student folders, I didn't see the transfer I had hoped for. While beginnings of sentences were in better shape than ever, I still saw random usage of capital letters and, more often than not, lowercase letters at the start of proper nouns.

Today I'd decided to pull a small group with the intent that what I taught in the small group would carry to others via a "small-group ripple effect." At the end of my small-group strategy lesson, I planned to have each member return to his or her writing table and teach a version to the people at the table. Though it was a risky move, I was excited to try it with the class and see what happened.

As soon as the six children joined me back in the meeting area, I began my strategy lesson. Beside me, I had an enlarged copy of a review I'd printed from TimetoPlayMag.com's website titled, "Beyblade: Metal Fusion." I'd highlighted the proper nouns in the first two columns of the review in yellow, as well as the capital letters that began each sentence in pink. The review begins:

MID-WORKSHOP TEACHING
Using Your Partner's Notes to Fix Your Writing

"Writers, I can tell you are hard at work, giving each other writing checkups and recording notes to give your partners ways to make their reviews easy to read. Remember, once you have had your checkup and received a prescription, be sure to get going on those doctor's orders! Use your partner's notes and your editing checklist to fix up your review. And just like you've made sure to be thorough when looking across your partner's piece, make sure to be thorough. When editing your own work, check all the way down the page, and across all the pages of your review, doing everything you can to fix it up!"

As Students Continue Working . . .

"Writers, I notice that many of you are working especially hard to fix up your spelling, making sure your words are easier to read. I want to teach you that one way writers spell the best they can is to try it two ways. You can write the word two different ways: try one way using all you know about how words work, and then close your eyes and picture how that word looks when you read it in a book or see it on a page. Try to spell it both ways, then look at each carefully to decide which one looks right. Circle it and move on to the next word!"

The phenomenon returns. Hasbro's Beyblade was a huge hit, taking the concept of customizable battling tops to a whole new level and spawning entertainment, competition, and a worldwide hit.

(continues)

Hasbro's one-time hit Beyblade is making a comeback with many major design improvements to engage a whole new generation of kids. The Beyblade: Metal Fusion battling top toy line encourages kids to collect, customize, and compete like never before with a new metal gear system and the introduction of an online virtual battle component.

"Writers, you have eagle eyes that are always on the lookout to make sure the beginnings of your sentences are capitalized. Look at this writer who wrote about Beyblades. He used his eagle eye to check and make certain his sentences all began with capital letters as well," I said, and I gestured quickly to each of the pink highlighted capital letters I'd marked up as the students nodded and checked with me.

"Take a moment, though, and look at the words I highlighted in yellow. Those words have capital letters at their beginning, too, and they certainly do not begin his sentences. And, I'll tell you this, these capital letters are not mistakes! Study those words, and ask yourself why you think those words all start with capital letters. Then later, I said, "Turn and tell your partner your thinking," I added after I'd given the group a few moments to study the piece and think.

Paula turned to her partner and said, "It's capital because it's the name of the toy—like my name is Paula so my P gets a capital, and its name is Bey-something so its name gets a capital."

I stopped the group. "Paula, tell the rest of this group what you just told Alejandro," I said. Paula repeated what she'd said, and I nodded along. "That's exactly why this writer used capital letters on those words. It's because it's the toy's proper name—just the same as if I wrote my name or you wrote your name. Check your writing right now. Reread it and check for places where you write the thing or the place that you are reviewing. Is it capitalized even if it isn't the beginning of the sentence? And fix it, fix it, fix it. Go!"

I moved quickly from student to student, coaching and guiding as needed, making sure that the focus was on rereading and finding proper nouns. I was not looking for instantaneous perfection, only for a lifted level of understanding that proper nouns get proper attention. Most of the writers in the group were well prepared, and within a few moments, the green editing pens had found more than one place to strike through and capitalize the proper nouns. Some of the students had even found places where their sentences needed a capital.

After five minutes of coaching and editing, I gathered the group back together and said, "You are now special proper noun agents and have a mission! Your mission, should you choose to accept it, is to return to your table and teach the other people at your table about how the names of things and the names of places that they are writing about need capital letters—even if they are not at the beginning of a sentence. If it is a thing's or a place's name, it needs a capital letter!"

I handed out copies of the review to each student, and once they'd accepted the mission, I nodded for them to go and teach the other writers at the tables. As they went off, I moved from table to table, gently coaching in as needed, but mostly watching and listening as the agents shared their knowledge with others.

Fixing Up Multiple Pieces for Publication

Create a drumroll for the next day's celebration, and have students fix up more pieces of writing from their folders.

I called students back to the meeting area for the share, asking that they each bring along their checklist, writing folder, and editing pen. I ushered students to settle quickly so that we would have ample time for our share session. I began by announcing news for the next day. "Tomorrow we will have a mini-celebration, and the hard work you did today will help us prepare for publishing, making sure that your reviews are easy to read and ready to share with the world!" I announced. The children were delighted by the news of a writing celebration.

I continued, "The work you did during today's workshop is the kind of work that writers in the world do every day. But, I'd like to remind you that writers get better at this kind of work when they check *all* of their writing—not just one piece, but every piece in their folder. This way, each of *you* will become the kind of writers who thinks carefully about your work and takes the time to make sure your pieces are ready for the eyes of readers." I spoke these words with intention, communicating the power first-graders hold to become purposeful writers.

"So, how about a very big challenge? Are you up for it?" I prodded.

"Yeah! Bring it on!" Dalton called out, playfully. The children giggled and joined in.

"Well, then, seeing that you are ready for some more big, important work, how about if instead of just stopping after fixing up one piece, you dive right back into your folders and spend the rest of our share time showing off all you know about fixing up your work? Give yourself a checkup to make *lots* of reviews the best they can be!" Then, motioning for students to ready their materials, I called out, "Clipboards?"

"Check!" the class asserted.

"Editing pens?" I quizzed.

"Check!" they returned.

"Another review?"

Students scrambled to take out another piece of writing to edit. "Check!"

"Get going, doctors! Fix it up!" As the students returned to edit a second piece, I moved in to work alongside students who would need additional guidance and support.

Making Anthologies
A Celebration

ear Teachers,

Today is a day for celebration, because it marks the end of the second bend of this unit. In place of a full plan for the day, this letter presents a possibility for some instructional fanfare around the occasion, but ultimately, you'll make your own decisions about how to close this bend based on the context of your own classroom. During yesterday's session, students worked in partnerships to give each other a writing checkup, finding parts to fix up as they readied a selected review for today's publishing celebration. Likely, your students sat, revision pen in hand, working hard to edit their work as best they could, following doctor's orders!

Today's session provides you with an opportunity for children to collaboratively publish anthologies. Perhaps writers will work in pairs, or small groups, clustered together based on a common topic or theme to share a series of reviews. For example, you might have students put together an anthology of popular video games or movies. Or, writers who have reviewed favorite vacation destinations might work together to publish a travel guide. You might decide to bring in published examples of such anthologies—such as a Zagat guide or a Fodor's travel book—sharing with your children ways that review writers in the world do this work every day!

MINILESSON

Your connection will congratulate writers on the hard work they've done across this unit, drawing from all they've learned to make their pieces not only convincing, but also easy to read—after all, if reviews are meant to convince readers, it goes without question that it'll be important for these reviews to be clear. Then, share that the reviews that students have written across the class remind you of the collections of reviews that writers in the world put together. You'll probably choose to show them specific examples of review anthologies.

This sets you up to deliver today's teaching point. As you know, teaching points are designed to present children with not only the larger skill of *what* writers do but also an explicit strategy to explain *how* writers do this work. This language makes your teaching replicable, so children are better able to transfer the strategy to their own independent practice. You might phrase your teaching point as follows: "Today I want to teach you that review writers publish anthologies of pieces that go together. Reviewers think, 'Who in the world might need to read this review? What is this review helping people do?' in order to decide what kind of anthology to create."

You'll demonstrate this strategy using your own review, perhaps looking back over your review of Pinkberry and thinking aloud about who might need to read it. "Hmmm . . . maybe this review will be helpful for people who want to know about ice cream places." Then, broadening the focus to model ways to encompass a larger audience, you might continue, "Or maybe, people who are curious about where to go for desserts should read this review. This could even go together with reviews about restaurants so readers can choose from all kinds of places to eat."

During the active engagement, prompt students to reflect on their chosen review and think, "Who in the world might need to read this review? What is this review helping people do?" Perhaps, this will help children get at the larger themes, such as, "This review is for people who want to see a good movie," or, "This review is for people who are hungry and want to go to a restaurant." Prompt students to share these ideas with partners on the rug. With students seated in the meeting area, you'll have the opportunity to move among writers quickly to offer support as needed. Then, record a list of the main topics on which students have written, asking your young reviewers to hold up their piece as you record names quickly beneath simple headings, such as "Food," "Movies," and "Video Games." In this way, you can form possible class anthologies. These groups will work together to fancy up their anthologies before sharing them with the class.

Rather than sending your children off to work at tables, you'll ask students to meet with their group (even if that group is limited to a pair of writers), convening in small circles in or around the meeting area. You'll prompt students to share their writing with each other and to ultimately decide what to entitle their group's anthology. As you move between groups, you'll coach students to think, "What is the same about all of these reviews? How can we write a catchy title that will get people to understand what these reviews are mostly about?" This way, you'll not only help children compose titles far flashier than "Food" but you'll also work toward supporting first-graders with identifying the main topic and describing the connection between two ideas or pieces of information—a standard for reading informational texts set forth by the Common Core (CCSS RI. 1.2, 1.3).

Signal for groups to move back to tables once they have determined a fitting title, and ask children to work together to design a cover page for their anthologies.

CONFERRING AND SMALL-GROUP WORK

You'll likely focus the small-group work you do today on coaching students as they prepare for the celebration share. You may decide to teach students to decide on a way to grab people's attention, perhaps asking a question that will lead to a "Yes, tell me more!" response. Or, you may facilitate groups as they rehearse together, offering lean prompts as needed, such as, "Speak louder" or "Tell us more!" Likewise, you may help students find a line or two to share aloud, reading a bit from each review to offer their audience a sneak peek and supplying students with Post-it notes to mark the part they'll share. Don't worry if you feel these presentations are far from smooth or perfectly ironed out. Today you're providing students with a quick taste for the work they'll return to at the end of the next bend.

MID-WORKSHOP TEACHING

To prepare for today's celebration, you may voice over to students, as they quickly finish their covers, that each group will have a chance to share its anthology with the rest of the class, giving a little commercial to convince everyone to read it. Guide students to plan by recalling the way they wrote catchy leads for their information books: asking a question to grab their attention and telling what the book is all about. Then, prompt groups to prepare and practice their "commercial" together, rehearsing and ad-libbing their introduction aloud.

SHARE

For today's share, you'll ask students to come to the meeting area with their group, each holding on to their own review, and one student holding the cover, all of which you'll bind together after each group presents.

In the spirit of celebration, you'll give each group the spotlight to perform their commercial, giving a short pitch to coax their audience to read on. After which, you'll collect the pages, stapling the anthology together, and place it into a newly labeled "Reviews" bin in the classroom library.

You'll be sure to congratulate your writers for their impressive work with publishing reviews that others can now read, helping make choices about movies, restaurants, toys, and games by using the opinions they've passionately shared.

Have fun!

Lucy, Celena, and Liz

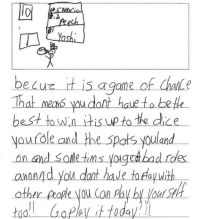

FIG. 13–1   Leander's review includes oganized pages, reasons and examples, transitions, and a sense of closure.

Leander's Published Review

Mario Party 4 (**** four stars)

Mario Party 4 is a great family game for every family. You will like it better than any shooter game and your parents will be glad that it is a friendly game, not a violent game. It is rated E so all kids can play, but not babies.

Mario Party 4 is a good game because it is a LOT of fun! There are a lot of mini games you play during the real game. One fun mini game is Squirt Alert. You have to be the first person to fill the water balloon up to win the coins.

Did you know you can pick the character you want when you play Mario Party 4? It's true! Yoshi is a good character to choose because he drives fast. Mario is a good choice too. Don't be Peach because she isn't very fast when you play the mini games. A good tip to know is that you should be able to tap buttons fast because that will help you win the game and win the stars.

Another reason you will like Mario Party is because it is easy. It is a little like Monopoly but with video games! Even little kids can play. When I play with my parents I always win but my mom is pretty good too. I can beat my brother too but not all the mini games.

You will like Mario Party because it is a game of chance. That means that you don't have to be the best to win, it is up to the dice you roll and the spots you land on and sometimes you get bad rolls. Annnnnnd, you don't have to play with other people, you can play it all by yourself too!! Go play it today!!!

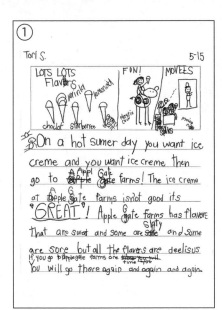

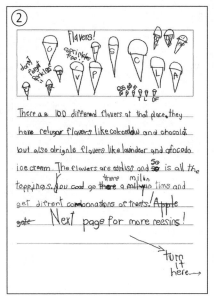

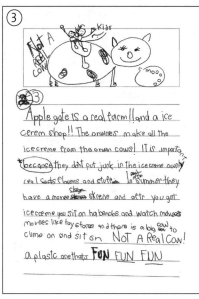

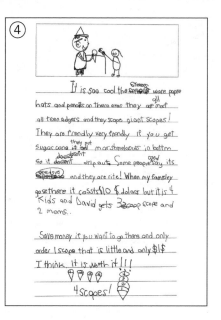

FIG. 13–2   Tori's review makes her revision and editing work very clear.

Tori's Published Review

On a hot summer day you want ice cream and you want ice cream then go to Apple Gate Farms! The ice cream at Apple Gate Farms isn't good—it's GREAT! Apple Gate Farms has flavors that are sweet and some are salty and some are sour but all of the flavors are delicious. If you go to Applegate Farms one time, you will go again and again.

There are 100 different flavors at that place. They have regular flavors like cookie dough and chocolate but also original flavors like lavender and avocado ice cream. The flavors are endless and so is all the toppings. You could go there a million times and get different combinations of treats!

Apple Gate is a real farm and an ice cream shop!! The owners make all the ice cream from their own cows! It is important because they don't put junk in the ice cream only real flavors and stuff. In the summer they have a movie screen and after you get ice cream you sit on hay benches and watch movies like Toy Story and there is a big cow to climb on and sit on—NOT A REAL COW!—A plastic one that's FUN FUN FUN.

It is so cool that the servers wear paper hats and pencils on their ears. They are almost all teenagers and they scoop the ice cream in giant scoops! They are friendly, very friendly. If you get a sugar cone they put marshmallows in the bottom so it doesn't drip out. Some people could say it's expensive and they are right! When my family goes it costs $10.00 but it is four kids and David gets 3 scoops and 2 moms.

Save money if you want to go there and only order 1 scoop that is little and only $1.00 I think. It is worth it!!!

Using All You Know to Write Book Reviews

IN THIS SESSION, you'll teach students that writers write book reviews to recommend titles and authors that they believe others should read.

GETTING READY

✔ Opinion Writing Checklist, Grades 1and 2 (see Teaching)

✔ "Convince Your Reader!" chart, created in Session 8 (see Teaching)

✔ *I Am Invited to a Party* by Mo Willems, or other familiar read-aloud to use to write a review (see Teaching)

✔ Students' independent reading book baggies (see Active Engagement)

IT WILL COME AS NO SURPRISE that we begin this final bend in the unit by asking writers to draw on all that they have learned to jump in and begin writing a slightly new kind of thing—in this case, book reviews. Is this not a habit we should all cultivate, bringing what we know to bear on a new situation? By this time in the unit, children are hopefully feeling more at home in the reviewer stance. Enjoy letting them revel in the feeling that there is a willing and eager audience for their opinions! Part of becoming a writer is realizing what it is that you have to say matters to the world.

On the first day of this unit children came to the meeting area with shoeboxes full of collections tucked snugly under their arms, and in that same way, today we ask them to come to the meeting area with baggies of books tucked under their arms. Just as back then they judged the coins or candy wrappers or erasers from their collections—comparing, ranking, studying, choosing favorites—today they'll judge the books in their baggies, developing their opinions in writing.

After choosing their favorites, you'll show children how to use all they have learned to write reviews, convincing others to read the book. Let children take the lead in this work, as this will give you an opportunity to see what they understand about the structure of reviews.

This session serves as a rallying call, a time to build excitement around the big and important work of writing about reading. The book reviews your writers begin today will serve as the start for literary essays they will write in years ahead.

COMMON CORE STATE STANDARDS: W.1.1, W.1.3, W.2.1, RL.1.1, RL.1.2, RL.1.3, RL.1.9, SL.1.1, L.1.1, L.1.2

Using All You Know to Write Book Reviews

CONNECTION

To generate enthusiasm around writing book reviews, tell a story about how helpful a book recommendation was in helping you select a new book to read.

I asked students to come over to the meeting area with their reading baggies in hand. Then, I asked them to sit on top of their baggies, so as to avoid any distraction. Once everyone had settled, I began with a story.

"Yesterday afternoon, I went to the library. I had just finished a great book, and I needed to return it to borrow another. But, as I was browsing the shelves, poring over title after title, I began to feel a little bit lost. How would I *ever* find the right book to read? There were thousands to choose from! But do you know what happened next?" I looked across the rug, as little faces leaned in, hanging on my next word.

"The librarian tiptoed over to me, and she whispered in my ear." Then, cupping my hands around my mouth, I mimicked, "'It looks as though you're searching for a good book to read. Well, I know a magnificent book that you might never want to put down! It's called *The Last of the Really Great Whangdoodles*, and if you liked *Charlie and the Chocolate Factory*,' she said, pointing at the book in my hand, 'then I know you'll like this story, too! It's filled with adventure and magic and it teaches an important lesson as well.'"

Then I moved from my storytelling to address the class, "The librarian helped me decide on a book to read. She gave me a recommendation, telling me about a book she really liked. You know, this is exactly the kind of thing I think you are ready to do in writing workshop! You've been hard at work writing reviews of movies and games and restaurants, even vacation places! But, what if we take on the very important, and very helpful, job of writing reviews of books and authors? Just like the librarian recommended a book to me, we can write book reviews that tell people about the books you love the most, convincing people to read them, too!" The boys and girls enthusiastically agreed to the proposal.

❖ **Name the teaching point.**

"Today I want to teach you that review writers write book reviews to recommend titles and authors they believe others should read. You can use all you already know about writing reviews to convince people to agree with your opinion."

Having the children sit on their baggies is one way we've found that keeps the materials they need close at hand but out of mind. While there are sometimes giggles the first time we ask children to do this, it is an efficient and effective way to keep the tools we want children to engage with close, but not distractive. If you have a child who refuses or is uncomfortable, of course, putting the books behind their back or to the side works too.

In math, you teach adding and subtracting by asking youngsters to hold math manipulatives. The concrete cubes help children grasp complicated concepts. When asking students to rank and review books, it's helpful for them to hold the books in their hands.

Children love hearing little stories from your life—and the stories about you as a reader have special payoff.

TEACHING

Channel students to reflect on all that they know about how to write convincing reviews.

"You already know so much about sharing the opinions you have about all kinds of things," I gestured toward the topic choice chart. Then I continued, gesturing toward the Opinion Writing Checklist, Grades 1 and 2, and the "Convince Your Reader!" charts, "and about writing reviews that really get people to trust you and follow your advice. I bet I don't even have to sit here and teach you about it all over again. Instead, you could probably teach *me* how to write reviews that are really convincing!" The boys and girls began to giggle and nod. "Right now, list across your fingers everything you know about writing reviews."

I gave the students a moment to work independently, watching as they held out fingers, counting out strategies. "Put a thumb up if you think you've got what it takes to teach me about writing convincing reviews." Kids quickly signaled back. "When I point toward you, will you say one smart thing you know about writing reviews? What do review writers do to convince their readers? Teach me!" I pointed toward Katerina first.

You may decide to have a mini version of the review chart that you've created previously with you so that as you listen to children share their thinking; you can give a quick gesture toward the strategy. Or, if there is a bit of a stall in children recalling what they know, you can gesture toward the chart to get the thinking started.

Opinion Writing Checklist

	Grade 1	NOT YET	STARTING TO	YES!	Grade 2	NOT YET	STARTING TO	YES!
	Structure				**Structure**			
Overall	I wrote my opinion or my likes and dislikes and said why.	☐	☐	☐	I wrote my opinion or my likes and dislikes and gave reasons for my opinion.	☐	☐	☐
Lead	I wrote a beginning in which I got readers' attention. I named the topic or text I was writing about and gave my opinion.	☐	☐	☐	I wrote a beginning in which I not only gave my opinion, but also set readers up to expect that my writing would try to convince them of it.	☐	☐	☐
Transitions	I said more about my opinion and used words such as *and* and *because*.	☐	☐	☐	I connected parts of my piece using words such as *also, another,* and *because*.	☐	☐	☐
Ending	I wrote an ending for my piece.	☐	☐	☐	I wrote an ending in which I reminded readers of my opinion.	☐	☐	☐
Organization	I wrote a part where I got readers' attention and a part where I said more.	☐	☐	☐	My piece had different parts; I wrote a lot of lines for each part.	☐	☐	☐
	Development				**Development**			
Elaboration	I wrote at least one reason for my opinion.	☐	☐	☐	I wrote at least two reasons and wrote at least a few sentences about each one.	☐	☐	☐
Craft	I used labels and words to give details.	☐	☐	☐	I chose words that would make readers agree with my opinion.	☐	☐	☐
	Language Conventions				**Language Conventions**			
Spelling	I used all I knew about words and chunks of words (*at, op, it,* etc.) to help me spell.	☐	☐	☐	To spell a word, I used what I knew about spelling patterns (*tion, er, ly,* etc.).	☐	☐	☐
	I spelled all the word wall words right and used the word wall to help me spell other words.	☐	☐	☐	I spelled all of the word wall words correctly and used the word wall to help me figure out how to spell other words.	☐	☐	☐

"Tell why they like it! Give reasons. And not just one. A lot of 'em," Katerina explained.

I nodded. "Impressive. And so important!" I gestured toward another student.

"You can give it stars to show how much you like it. Five stars is the best!"

"You can teach a little bit about it so people know what it is. Like maybe they won't know what Angry Birds is, so you have to explain it," Leander stated.

"So helpful! Yes, yes, yes!" I replied, before gesturing toward another child.

"You can tell a story about one time when you went there," Roselyn said back.

"Hmm . . . why do review writers do that?" I prodded.

"Because it'll make people want to go, too. Like, if you say, I went there and it was so much fun, then it might make them want to go have fun there," Roselyn responded.

"Oh, you know what? The librarian did that when she was recommending the book to me. She told me about the time she was reading it on the train, and she was so surprised by something that happens in the middle, she almost fell out of her seat! That definitely got me curious about it, and I can't wait to read it and find out what happens!" I shared. "My goodness! You really *can* teach a lot about writing convincing reviews. That's important because you'll need to use these smart strategies when you write book reviews."

Model planning and writing a book review, using strategies students have named for you.

"Let me see if I can use some of those smart strategies to plan a book review. Well, I know the exact book I'd like to recommend first!" I moved toward the bookshelf and picked up a familiar read-aloud, one that the class adored. "This is one of our favorite picture books. But what could we say about this book to convince others to agree with us? What reasons and details could we include?" I paused, as if to think. "Oh, I know what I could say in a review of this book. I could start it like this." I planned aloud:

> *I Am Invited to a Party is one of the funniest books you'll ever read! Mo Willems is a hilarious author, and every page of this story will make you laugh.*

"I better give details to show why it's so funny," I reflected. Then, I continued:

> Elephant and Piggie dress up in the wackiest outfits! Also, Elephant keeps changing his mind about what they should wear to the party!

If time is short and you want to tighten your minilesson, you could always recruit children to coauthor this review, turning it into the active engagement section. Become accustomed to noting when minilessons have a two-part teaching or active engagement section, as these can usually be trimmed.

"I could even tell a little story about a time when we read this book," I added:

> One time, our class read this story together, and we laughed so hard that our bellies hurt!

"But wait, earlier Katerina said that we can't just give one reason. It's more convincing to include lots of reasons. Let me say more:"

> Another reason why you should read this book is because the illustrations are so detailed. Mo Willems is a great artist. His pictures show exactly how the characters are feeling in each scene. I recommend this book to readers who like silly stories.

I turned my attention back to the class. "Did you notice how I made sure to include my opinion about the book and reasons why I feel this way? I even made sure to add details to support my reasons. Do you think if I wrote this in my book review, it would convince the other first-grade classes to want to read this story, too?" The kids agreed emphatically.

ACTIVE ENGAGEMENT

Give students an opportunity to plan a book review using one of their independent reading books.

"Take out your reading baggies. Look through your books and decide which book you think is the best. And when you've chosen your favorite, think to yourself, 'Why is this book so great? What can I say to convince other people to read it?' Then you can think of all you know that can help you write and persuade others to read this book. After you've planned in your head for a moment, rehearse with your partner what you might say in a book review. What reasons will you give? What details will you share?" I gestured for students to begin thinking and planning as I moved in to coach, as needed.

LINK

Remind students that they can use all that they know about writing persuasive reviews to write book reviews.

"So, writers, remember that whenever you are writing, you can always use everything you know to help you. When you write book reviews, you can include reasons and details, important information, comparisons, and maybe even a little story just as you've been doing in your reviews of restaurants, movies, video games, and toys.

"I've stocked the writing center with more review paper so you can get started on this work right away. Perhaps you'll decide to write your first review about the book from your reading baggy. Or maybe you'll decide to write a review about another book you love. However you begin, you'll want to make sure to use the charts in our room to help make your reviews really convincing, right from the start! And, as always, if you finish one review you can either revise your work or move on to write other reviews. Okay, go ahead and get started."

To keep your teaching well paced, you'll choose time to compose aloud, writing "in the air" rather than on paper.

Remember to record your words in writing outside of your lesson so that you're able to return to this demonstration piece in future minilessons, small groups, and conferences.

Planning for Book Reviews Using Strategies from Narrative and Information Writing

TODAY, THOUGH THE FOCUS of the minilesson encouraged students to transfer all they know about reviews to this new kind of review, you will no doubt find writers who forget to do that.

The first sign of this will be that some children neglect to plan at all. Benjamin was one such writer. Pulling close to him, I said, "Benjamin, I see you've already jumped into writing your review. Tell me your plans for your writing," I began.

"I'm writing about my *Fish!* book. It's my favorite, and I think other kids should read it, too."

"Okay, Benjamin, you just told me what you have written so far, and I actually want to hear your plan for your writing."

He giggled. "I got my paper and I got my idea, then I wrote my idea."

"So you gathered all the tools that you'd need, sat down, and made your writing space ready. Tell me, though, what is your plan for your writing?"

"Well, I just know my words," Benjamin said.

"Oh! Great, tell me what you're planning to write," I nudged. "What are your words?"

"Okay. I want to write, '*Fish!* is the best book in the whole library because it is full of fish facts and . . .'" Ben's voice trailed off. I waited, not saying a word, just listening and interested. "And . . ." he stammered again, "and . . . and . . . and *Fish!* has good pictures in it, too. And . . ." again, he paused. After a bit longer he continued, "And it tells about fish eggs . . .'"

"Benjamin, can I stop you for a moment and teach you something?" He nodded, so I began. "I think that you forgot that whenever you write, it helps to first make a plan for writing. When you wrote information books and way back when you wrote Small Moment stories, you planned those pieces before you wrote them. You probably planned those pieces by touching each page and saying what you would write, or by using your fingers to say your ideas for each part of your book. That same planning that you did as a story writer and an information writer—it works as a review writer, too! Review writers can't just jump right into their reviews. They have to plan their reviews first. Otherwise, reviews end up being a big long list of reason after reason. That won't work!"

Benjamin smiled a little, so I pressed on, exaggerating my example, "I mean, if you keep writing like that we will have to roll your writing like a scroll, and when someone goes to read it they'll have to unroll it all down the hallway. It will just be list after list after list. That's not a review! You certainly don't want that, do you?" Benjamin giggled.

(continues)

MID-WORKSHOP TEACHING **Review Writers Take Their Audience into Account When Writing**

I called for the students to take a brief hiatus from their writing. "Writers, I want to teach you that review writers have to think carefully about who their reviews are for to make sure they include information that will be important for those readers. You can think, 'Is this review for people who know about this book or this author already? Or is this review for people who don't know anything about this kind of book?' If your audience already knows about the author, or the topic, or the characters, you can make comparisons to show how this book is the same or different from other books just like it. But, if your audience doesn't know anything about the book, you'll want to include information that introduces them to the book."

"Benjamin, I suggest that you remember what you already know and use it as a review writer today and every single time you write. You know lots of ways to plan. Right here and right now, while I'm listening, will you decide which way you'll plan your review? And then, while I'm listening and watching, will you start to plan your review?"

"Okay, I'll try planning with my paper and touching each page."

"That's definitely one way writers plan. Benjamin, remember, even though you are excited to write your review, planning is very important to all writers, whether they are writing stories or information books or reviews. Without a plan, writers can get out of control and can just keep listing and listing their reasons and never have an ending. Writing without planning is like jumping out of an airplane and forgetting to take your parachute! Don't forget to plan, Benjamin. And remember, there are different ways to plan, use the one that works best for you every time!"

Making Comparisons in Book Reviews

Teach students that they can use comparisons to help persuade their readers to read the book they are reviewing.

"Today you worked hard writing reviews to recommend books you love. Many of them were favorites from your own baggies; others wrote about favorite read-aloud books from our class; some of you even wrote about books you love from home. I want to remind you that review writers sometimes make comparisons to explain their opinions. This helps make reviews even more convincing. If I made a comparison in a book review about *I Am Invited to a Party*, I might say:

> If you liked the book, **There Is a Bird on Your Head**, then you'll like **I Am Invited to a Party** because they are both silly stories about Elephant and Piggie. I think **I Am Invited to a Party** is even funnier than **There Is a Bird on Your Head** because of all the silly clothes they wear in this book.

"You can make a comparison to show how two books are the same or different. You can also explain how one is better than another. You might say, 'If you liked . . . then you'll like . . . because . . .' or 'I think . . . is more . . . because . . .' to explain which you prefer. You might even use *better* and *best* words like: *funnier* and *funniest*, or *scarier* and *scariest*, or *cooler* and *coolest* to describe what you think about each book."

Don't Spill the Beans!
Giving Sneak Peek Summaries

IN THIS SESSION, you'll teach students that book review writers give a sneak peek summary and are careful not to give away too many details about the book.

GETTING READY

✔ Your own book review written with two different beginnings, one that gives away too much information and one that does not, enlarged on chart paper (see Teaching)

✔ Chart paper, marker (see Teaching)

✔ Books that students wrote reviews about in the previous day's writing workshop (see Active Engagement)

COMMON CORE STATE STANDARDS: W.1.1, W.1.5, RL.1.1, RL.1.2, RL.1.3, SL.1.1, SL.1.3, L.1.1, L.1.2

I F EVER YOU FEEL YOUR TEACHING IS GROWING BORING OR LIFELESS, or you are at a loss for what to teach that feels important and true, I have two suggestions for you that have never yet failed me.

One is this: try writing in the genre in which you are asking your children to write. The writing you produce does not need to be a masterpiece, and it certainly does not need to be long. For this unit, you could ask yourself to write a quick review of another book you've read, one you'd be willing to post on, say, Amazon.com® or another book-friendly site. If you write with an awareness of the process you are undertaking and the questions and struggles and moves you make, I promise you will find understandings that you can use to bring vitality and strength to your teaching. Share with your students what you have struggled with, what you've found, and what you've tried that doesn't work. Show them your drafts and and false starts, even if they are only a sentence or a phrase. They will see your investment and your honest attempts to work through the same struggles they are having, and these shared experiences will bring them confidence and insight.

Here is the other suggestion: read a stack of published pieces of writing in the genre in which you are asking children to write. Analyze your own reactions to them. Are they working on you? What do the professionals in this area do that you could teach children to do? What seem to be the tricks of the trade, the structures and the conventions of the genre that are a bit more particular than the ideas that come to mind first? What are the qualities that make one piece in this genre better than another? For this unit, and for this bend in particular, you could read from periodicals that review literature as their main endeavor—*Horn Book, Kirkus Review,* and others. Or, you could read from book websites that allow for customer reviews and from reader blogs to see what reviewers there do that is worthy of teaching your children. If you prefer, you could even step outside the world of books and read reviews of any sort of product or event. There is much to be learned from a great customer review of a strapless dress or of a power tool or of a recipe for tuna casserole—reading them closely to think, "What makes this review so compelling? How can I do that in my own writing?"

For this bend in this unit (as for all of the bends in all of our units) we took these suggestions. When we pooled our experiences with those of the teachers with whom we work, we concluded that the insight that would most transform children's thinking about their writing and their writing itself, was that reviewers include a particular kind of description of what they are reviewing—one that does not spoil the suspense or ruin the surprises. This is an insider convention—one that no good review should do without. And, it is no small detail in the development of a writer. Learning to consider one's audience, learning to create a respectful relationship with one's reader, anticipating her reactions and concerns, is a writing skill that can take a lifetime to develop.

"Reviewers include a particular kind of description of what they are reviewing—one that does not spoil the suspense or ruin the surprises."

So, try teaching this session, or, better yet, go write, go read, and then go teach your own newly invented session, tailored from your own experiences and tailored for your own children. In that case, you can simply keep the ideas in this session in your back pocket, to pull out if you think they could help you as you work with small groups or with individual children in conferences.

Don't Spill the Beans!

Giving Sneak Peek Summaries

CONNECTION

Respond to something in students' writing so far, offering feedback about something they could change that would improve the reader's experience.

I called students to the meeting area, asking them to bring the book they wrote their first review about, and again instructing that they sit on top of it to get ready for our lesson. Then, I began, "Last night, I took each of your writing folders home with me. I was so excited to learn about the books you've recommended. I'm always on the lookout for new books to read! So, I sat down on my couch to read your book reviews. Except, as I was reading some of your pieces, I realized there was a bit of a problem. You told *so* many details about your book that I felt like I *already* knew the whole story. Now I won't even need to read the book because I know just about *everything* that happens. If we are going to write book reviews that convince people to read the books we love, it'll be important to leave them feeling curious about the book so they'll want to read and find out more. We don't want them feeling like we've spoiled the surprise, do we? Reviewers are usually pretty careful not to do that!"

❖ **Name the teaching point.**

"Today I want to teach you that writers of book reviews give a sneak peek summary without giving everything away. One way to do this is to share only the most important things readers will need to know about the book and also a few things that will make them curious, but not the ending!"

TEACHING

Offer contrasting introductions to your review—one that spoils the surprise, one that does not. Ask children to decide which works best.

"I'll show you what I mean. Here is one way my review of the Elephant and Piggie book could start. I'll read it to you, and you see if it makes you want to read the book or if it says too much. After I've read it, think to yourself, 'Does this make me want to read the book?'" I held up a revision flap I had attached to the beginning of my review and began to read aloud:

◆ COACHING

It's likely that in their first tries to write book reviews, children worked hard to write all they know about their books. You may want to emphasize the delicate work of writing just enough but not too much in a summary.

Modeling the revision work you've done between writing workshops sends the message that you are a writer who works outside as well as inside the workshop. Don't be surprised when you find writers, even as little as your first-graders, who emulate you and come to the workshop with "in between" work they've created at home, on the bus, outside of workshop.

You should read **I Am Invited to a Party** because Elephant and Piggie don't know what kind of party it will be, and then they find out at the end that it's a fancy pool costume party.

I turned back toward the class and asked them to share their reactions to this summary.

"I heard a lot of you saying this introduction did *not* make you want to read the book—it gave it all away! So let me try again." I tore off the first revision flap and got a new, blank one and started again:

I Am Invited to a Party is about an elephant named Gerald and his friend Piggie.

"I don't think I've told too much yet, do you? Next, I'd better tell the reader something interesting, something to make her curious and make her want to read—like what the problem or adventure is. I need to explain the situation in the book."

In this story, they are getting ready to go to a party. But there's a big problem! They don't know what kind of party it will be, so they can't decide what to wear!

"I know that one way to leave readers feeling curious is to ask a question that makes them wonder. And I have to remember not to answer it! I can include a question so they'll have to read to find out the answer." I returned to the review to tack on:

What kind of party will it be? Will Gerald and Piggie figure out what to wear? You'll have to read this book to find out!

"Now I'll read this whole new introduction to you—will you help me by letting me know if it convinces you to read this book? Does this version make you a little curious?" Then, with my revision flap in hand, I reread the whole beginning, aloud. Students nodded and chattered to let me know this one worked better.

Debrief, describing what you've done that students can also do.

"Did you notice how in my second try—the version that worked—I made sure not to give away the whole book? I didn't tell the ending since I knew that would not make my reader want to read it! Instead, I gave a sneak peek. I introduced the *characters*. I explained the *situation* in the story. Then, I asked a *question* to make the reader wonder. You could try that, too!" I flipped to a new page of chart paper and jotted a quick chart listing the steps of writing a book review introduction.

You'll want to make your process transparent to help children replicate it independently. Move between writing and thinking aloud to demonstrate strategies for planning and elaboration.

- Introduce the characters or topic.
- Explain the situation or share an interesting fact.
- Ask a question.

ACTIVE ENGAGEMENT

Ask students to plan aloud a sneak peek introduction they will add to their own reviews to make readers curious.

"Yesterday, each of you began writing a review of a book. Some of you even moved on to start writing another! Now, let's go back and think about what will be important to say in your sneak peek at the beginning of each of your reviews. Look at your writing and look at the book and think of what you could say as a sneak peek that doesn't give away the ending." I moved in to coach students, helping them talk through what they planned to say.

I knelt beside Ashley as she gazed at the cover of her book. I whispered, "Who's this story about?"

"Olivia," she whispered back.

Then, reading the title aloud, I echoed, "*Olivia Plants a Garden* is about a pig named Olivia." Then, I prompted Ashley to elaborate about the story. "Is there a problem in this story?"

She scrunched her nose and shook her head. "She plants a surprise plant at school."

"Oh! Olivia goes on an adventure in your story." Then again, I echoed this back to help Ashley understand the structure of the summary. "*Olivia Plants a Garden* is about a pig named Olivia, and in this story, she plants a special surprise at school."

You'll want to model this oral rehearsal with children, echoing their ideas in clear and structured ways as a means of supporting more focused and cohesive writing.

"Yeah, and she talks to the plant and sings to the plant to make it grow faster!" she went on.

"Oh! But don't give it all away! Make your reader wonder what will happen. I bet you can ask a question at the end of your sneak peek to make your reader guess!" I nudged.

"Will Olivia's plant ever grow? Read and find out!" Ashley composed.

"Oh, that question will definitely make readers wonder. Then, they'll have to find this book and read it," I cheered. "Say your whole sneak peek again to yourself to practice."

I moved on to coach a few other students along, as students worked independently. Then, I stopped the class.

Ask students to try their sneak peek on their partners, checking to see if their "writing" has the intended effect.

"Now will you turn and give your partner a sneak peek of your book to make sure you're not giving away too much? Say out loud the words you'll write in your review, then check to see if it makes your partner curious to read the book!" As partners rehearsed aloud, I listened in to coach writers along, at times echoing back their summary in more structured ways and prompting them to repeat it once more. Then, I reconvened the group to admire their work.

"You know, as I was listening in to your sneak peeks, it got me really curious about all of your books. I want to know what happens in the story and what else I'll learn from your information books! I'm going to have to find these books and read them. When you give a sneak peek of your book, it makes your reviews much more convincing."

LINK

Remind readers to use this strategy whenever they need it. In this case, remind them to entice readers by offering interesting information but not too much information.

"So, writers, remember that whenever you are writing book reviews, it's important to include a sneak peek summary that doesn't give it all away. You can share only the most important things readers will need to know about the book. You might even hook your readers with a question to make them wonder. If you forget what you need to do, just take a quick look back at the "Give a Sneak Peek" chart I just jotted up front. This way, you can convince others to read the books you recommend."

Giving writers the opportunity to orally rehearse again and again is key to supporting them in getting more on the page. Writing, like speaking, goes well when we have much to say. You may want to keep that in mind as the children rehearse today, and offer plenty of opportunities for oral rehearsal to happen. Then, as the children go off to write, voice over your expectations that just like the rich rehearsal in the room, you're expecting juicy words down the page.

Using All You Know to Write Persuasively Right from the Start

ONCE THE SMALL GROUP OF STUDENTS HAD GATHERED ON THE RUG, sitting around me with their writing folders and pens, I began.

"My grandma used to say, 'Never put off till tomorrow something you can do today,'" I said, and looked at the writers I'd gathered on the rug for today's small-group instruction. "I think it's the perfect advice I can give you as you begin to draft your book reviews.

"What she means is this: if you know how to do something, and you know that something needs to be done, then just do it! Right now. Even though you have written book reviews for only a day or so, you already know a lot about what goes inside a review. Don't wait until tomorrow to go back and revise and put in all you know it will need. Do it right now, as you draft your review. Use the charts to help you remember all the things review writers do to make their reviews persuasive. Get started."

The urgency in my voice ushered the students to begin writing immediately. I moved around to Jorge and quickly read what he had started, coaching in, "Oh! You already have your opinion and reasons. Check the chart. Choose another strategy to try as you keep writing."

I moved on without waiting to hear Jorge's choice, knowing I'd be back around soon to assess how he was using all he knew about review writing.

"Aiden," I whispered, "what are you using from the chart to make this review the best review you've written yet?"

Aiden cupped his hand to his mouth, leaned close, and whispered, "I'm hooking my reader with a catchy introduction!" He tapped the end of his pen onto his paper to show me his work."

"Remembering to start your review with an introduction is hard work, Aiden. You must feel proud of being such a thoughtful and detailed writer," I continued to whisper.

Aiden nodded and quickly flipped his pen back around to continue writing. "Don't spill the beans!" I reminded him and leaned back to move to the next student. I stole a quick glance back to Jorge's page to make sure he was writing and engaged. His pen was poised in the air, and he was studying the chart seriously, so I continued to another member of the group.

Before I said a word, Tori chirped, "I already have my intro. I heard you talk to Aiden, and I wrote mine. It says, 'Get the library pass from your teacher and go check out *A Pet for Petunia* because it is funny, funny, funny!'"

MID-WORKSHOP TEACHING
Don't Just Add More!: Revising to Subtract

"Writers, you're working so hard to make sure that your book reviews show off all you know about review writing. I want to remind you to use something else you know how to do. When writers revise, they can revise to add information. But they can also make decisions to revise and take *out* parts of their writing. Revision doesn't mean just add, add, add. You can also take away parts of your reviews that don't go, or don't make sense, or don't really convince. As you write and reread, be sure to stop and think, 'Does this go? Does this help convince readers?' If yes, keep it! But if not, revise by taking it out!"

"Tori, wow, well done," I said. "What are you planning to do next?" I gestured toward the chart. "State your opinion or make a comparison?" I inquired, hoping my questioning would serve as a guide for Tori as she continued to draft her review.

"I'm going to write my opinion, then give reasons and tell why *A Pet for Petunia* is better than other books," Tori said.

"Smart thinking, Tori. Back to it. Keep making decisions about the types of things you want to add when you write your review. Check the chart, and decide what else you need to include."

I moved back to Jorge and noticed that in a matter of minutes, he'd filled over a page. As I read, I saw evidence of many features inside his review. I leaned in and said, "Jorge, I think you've got the hang of this. I can see how you've done all sorts of things to convince your readers. You have your introduction." I tapped my finger to the first few lines of his page where he'd written a catchy lead, getting readers interested in reading his book. "I see you have a strong opinion and reasons to persuade your readers," I continued, and moved my finger to circle where he'd done this work. "Jorge, head back to your seat and keep writing! Use the chart when you need it. Make sure you remember to do this thoughtful work as you write other reviews, too!"

I saw that Jorge was able, without much coaching or guidance, to reference the chart and independently make decisions as he composed his review. There was no need for him to remain with the rest of the group, so I sent him back to allow more time with students who needed more guided practice and attention.

As I moved back and forth between the students I had kept with me on the rug, I continued to coach into their planning and drafting work, reminding them to draw from the chart and use all they know about review writing to write persuasively from the very start.

Giving Writing Checkups

Using Partners Purposefully

Teach students how to go to their partners with specific concerns about their writing, asking them to look at certain aspects of their work.

Before calling students over to the meeting area, I asked the class to place a Post-it note on their writing folders and to bring their folders and pens to their rug spot. Once the class had gathered, placing their materials down on the rug beside them, I began. "Writers, sometimes when you go to the doctor it is for a checkup, and sometimes, it's because something isn't feeling very good.

"You can think of your writing partner that same way. Sometimes you take your writing to your partner for a checkup. But other times, you can think, 'What part of my writing isn't feeling so good? Do I need to check it for capitals? For punctuation?' and then you can ask your partner to look at your writing for just that one thing.

"Then, after your partner has looked it over carefully, he or she can write you a prescription—a little note that reminds you of what you can do to make your writing feel (and look and sound) even better.

"Go ahead and get started. Partner 2, you'll start today. Ready? The doctors are . . . in!" The room was aflutter with checkups and doctors' orders. I monitored students to listen in, coach, and make plans for teaching.

Children are often more apt to find problems in the work of others before they identify it in their own. For this reason, the role of partnerships in peer editing is hugely supportive. By guiding students to review their partner's writing with a particular lens—capitals, word wall words, punctuation—rather than to edit haphazardly, children will be more successful in locating and correcting errors.

Not Too Long, Not Too Short!

Using Conjunctions

THINK BACK TO YOUR OWN LEARNING, be it lessons learned within academic walls or times outside the classroom—perhaps learning to drive a car, upload a file, or bake chocolate-chip cookies. Most likely, your road to success involved considerable approximation, engaging in activities and doing things *almost* right—hitting the car brake a bit too hard, having nothing at all appear on your screen, or leaving the cookies in the oven for a minute too long, burning the bottoms. These mistakes make us smarter and far more aware of how to get it right. A learner's approximations are a critical piece to long-term understanding.

Dr. Brian Cambourne tells us in *The Whole Story* (1988) that approximation is critical to learning—that we, as teachers, must allow for children to be risk takers and to congratulate them on the mistakes they make and to help them learn from those mistakes. He says approximation is one condition that sets learners up for success—whether it be mistakes in oral, read, or written language.

What a drag it would be if every time we tried something new, it came without effort or mishap! We'd surely have no stories to tell, no sense of accomplishment for our hard work. Instead, we'd be left with experiences that blend together with all the rest. It's with this same appreciation for risk taking and mistake making that you'll approach today's session, teaching youngsters to question all they know about sentence structure and to push forward to write more complex sentences.

Rest assured that your students' approximations, along with the guidance and support you provide, will foster a deeper understanding of this skill, along with a raised level of confidence for exploring this work as writers. You'll coach students to reread for sense and to revise for meaning and syntax, encouraging ongoing practice with sentence composition. As you embark on today's teaching, you'll want to hold tight to the adage, "No risk, no gain," expecting a classroom of risk takers who are empowered to question, revise, and yes, approximate.

Opinion writers know that to convince, one must provide reasons that support their claims. You may have noticed that while writers are incorporating reasons into their reviews,

IN THIS SESSION, you'll teach students that writers check their sentences to make sure that they are just right. If the sentences aren't, writers use punctuation marks, linking words, or other editing tools to make them just right.

GETTING READY

✔ Copy of the book, *Goldilocks and the Three Bears* (see Connection)

✔ "Is This Sentence Just Right?" list (see Teaching and Active Engagement)

✔ Student piece of persuasive writing (such as "Earrings") filled with run-on sentences using "and" and "then" as connectors, enlarged for students to see (see Teaching and Active Engagement)

✔ Craft sticks with different punctuation marks on them (see Teaching and Active Engagement)

✔ Short book review video clip (see Share)

✔ "Give a Sneak Peek!" list from Session 15 (see Share)

✔ Chart paper with the title "How to Give a Convincing Review" written across the top (see Share)

COMMON CORE STATE STANDARDS: W.1.1, W.1.5, W.2.1, RL.1.1, RL.1.2, SL.1.1, SL.1.2, SL.1.3, SL.1.4, SL.1.6, L.1.1.g,j, L.1.2.b,d,e; L.1.6, L.2.1.f

some students are apt to simply list these reasons, one right after another, while others use long, drawn-out sentences, connecting each with the word "and," so that down one page it reads as one run-on list of reasons. Today, you'll start children out by teaching a multi-step process for checking their work to revise these kinds of sentences. While you'll teach the first step in the process, you'll help students understand that all the steps across your process chart can help writers develop more thoughtfully constructed sentences that will both engage their readers and make their writing easier to read and understand.

Ready? Set? Approximate!

"As you embark on today's teaching, expect a classroom of risk takers who are empowered to question, revise, and approximate."

Not Too Long, Not Too Short!
Using Conjunctions

CONNECTION

Introduce the idea of being brave and choosy as writers, perhaps by offering up the example of Goldilocks searching for what was "just right" before making her decision.

"Class, last night I was thinking about the story of Goldilocks and the Three Bears. I was thinking about how even though Goldilocks was a bit naughty for going into the Bears' home and trying their things and breaking Baby Bear's chair, she isn't *just* naughty. We know, as readers, that characters—all people, really—are more than just one way. In this book, Goldilocks keeps trying and trying until she finds *exactly* what she wants. She isn't afraid to try something, then say, 'Nope, too big!' or 'Nah, not for me! Too small!'"

I moved on to offer students a contrasting example: "There are some people who aren't brave like that. There are people who make one decision and then refuse to ever change their mind. I certainly don't want to be that sort of person, especially as a writer! Instead, we can be like Goldilocks when we write—not *naughty* Goldilocks, but *brave* and *choosy* Goldilocks in that story."

❖ **Name the teaching point.**

"Today I want to teach you that writers check their writing to make sure that the sentences they've written are just how they want them to be. Writers reread each sentence and ask, 'Is my sentence too long? Is my sentence too short? Is it just right?' Then, writers use punctuation to break it apart or use linking words to connect ideas or edit it in other ways to make it just right."

TEACHING AND ACTIVE ENGAGEMENT

Introduce a list that will help students figure out whether their sentences are just right. Then show a sample of a book review that is full of sentences that are not just right.

"This list can help you figure out whether your sentences are just right, and then what to do if they are *not* just right." I pointed toward the easel, and read it aloud:

Sitting on my lap was a copy of Goldilocks and the Three Bears, *by James Marshall, one of the class's favorite read-aloud stories. We'd had whole-class discussions about Goldilocks and how she persevered, as well as how she'd learned an important lesson. The story had lived in our class in big ways, so I didn't shy away from using it today as a way to rally students to try the sophisticated work of editing for run-on sentences with something they already understood quite well, how to make "just right" decisions.*

Is This Sentence Just Right?

If a sentence . . .

- goes on and on and on, stop it earlier with punctuation.
- ends too soon, use AND, SO, or BUT to say more.
- gets confusing, say it in a different way.

"I found this review that a first-grader wrote last year. Let's pretend we are the author of it and revise it to make these sentences just right." I flipped to the page of chart paper where I had enlarged the review. "Let's start by rereading, like anytime we revise work. Reread along with me:

> I just read the book **Earrings** and you should read it too and it is so so good and you will love it. The little girl wants earrings and her mom says no and her dad says no and they keep saying no no no and she keeps saying why why why and she tells them she should have them and they say no no no and it goes on and on and on.
>
> It is a funny book! You will like it! You should read it. You should read it now. Go read it.

Before we'd even reached the end of the first paragraph, thumbs were waving in the air, and kids were up on their knees, eager to share ideas for the work to be done. "Are there sentences that are not just right?" I asked, leaving a space for students to form their thoughts, rather than chiming in right away to confirm their discoveries. I prompted partners to quickly turn to one another and share their musings.

"It's too long!" said voices from around the room.

Recruit writers to chime in as you revise sentences to make them just right.

I stared out to the sea of writers. "What should we do to make it just right? Partner 1, turn and tell your partner how we can fix it to make this sentence just right. How would you revise this sentence that we feel is too long?" The children turned quickly, and partners around the room began sharing revision plans. I walked toward the back of the meeting area, and knelt beside two partners already in the midst of revision talk.

"I'd add periods to fix it," said Rosa, turning to her partner.

"Where?" I nudged, asking her to again reread and think about a stopping point. "How do you know where punctuation marks should go? Explain your decision to your partner," I whispered in, coaching Rosa to say more.

I chose a student piece that mirrored the writing I had been observing across the class, using an unknown first-grader to teach students strategies for editing sentence structure.

> I just read the book Earrings and you should read it too and it is so so so good and you will love it The little girl wants earrings and her mom says no and her dad says no and they keep saying no no no and she keeps saying why why why and she tells them she should have them and they say no no no and it goes on and on. It is a funny book and you should read it You should read it now go read it!

FIG. 16–1 Writing from a child in another class can provide an opportunity for students to help you edit.

"Hmm . . ." Rosa pondered, her eyes moving back to the chart paper to reread the first part of the review. "I'd put a period maybe after '. . . and you should read it too.'"

"Try it," I said, and handed Rosa the punctuation stick and told her to come up front and try the work in front of the class.

I stopped the class and said, "Writers, Rosa reread the first part of this review and asked herself, 'Is it too long? Is it too short?' She decided that there are parts that go on and on. Watch as she makes them just right.

"How would you make this a just-right sentence—a sentence that doesn't go on and on and makes it too long?"

"Maybe here," Rosa said, holding the craft stick up to place a period at the end of ". . . you should read it too."

"Reread it to make sure it sounds just right, Rosa," I reminded, tapping on the third item on the list. Rosa read and nodded that she'd made the right decision. "So, do we need that 'and' to make the sentence keep going?" I questioned.

"No!" the class retorted, and Rosa crossed out "and," then added a period.

LINK

Send students off to work, reminding them of the questions they should be asking themselves.

"Keep going. When you continue rereading reviews, ask yourself if some sentences are too long or too short. Remember to be brave and choose as carefully as Goldilocks did. Ask yourself, 'Is this sentence too long? Is this sentence too short?' Then, you can fix the sentences. This is hard work and it will make you stronger as readers and writers."

To support engagement, as well as to make your teaching stick, it helps to create tools for children that make the work they are doing as writers more tangible. The craft stick I'd pulled from my own writing folder and given to Rosa had different end punctuation marks from which to choose: a period, a question mark, and an exclamation point.

As you coach into students' work, support approximations and thoughtfulness.

Following Up on Past Conferences

Making Sure Your Teaching Is Sticking

As I APPROACHED AUSTIN'S DESK, I looked back to the past few conferences we'd had, recalling that I'd focused on including details to further support his reasons. While Austin was keen to apply strategies I taught in the moment, I realized that I didn't see much evidence of my teaching sticking—that is, it wasn't apparent that Austin had carried those strategies forward in his writing, applying them across the pieces in his folder.

Taking this quick look back at the previous work I'd done with Austin helped me plot my course of action in today's conference. Instead of focusing on developing Austin's quality of writing, I decided to focus my teaching, as well as Austin's attention, on his writing behavior. I began, "The last time we met, you worked hard to make your reviews more convincing. You learned to add details to make your reasons even stronger. I'm interested to see where you've continued to do that work." I went on, "Show me where you've continued to add details to make your writing convincing. Take me on a tour of the places you've tried this since the last time we met."

Austin looked at me, then back down at the writing in front of him. After just a few moments, he began to finger through the various review pages tucked inside his folder. He looked back at me, and I gave him an encouraging smile. After a second pregnant pause, Austin looked bravely at me, admitting, "I don't think I have more places to show you."

I turned over my clipboard, pushing aside my conference notes, to have a heart-to-heart with Austin. "Austin, I think what I need to teach you today isn't *another* way to make your writing convincing. I think what's especially important to tell you about is how writers make sure to practice things again and again! You can use all the strategies you know in every one of your pieces, even when I'm not here beside you. You *know* how to do this work. I see it here," I said, pointing to a revision strip in his booklet, "and here," I continued. "But, it feels like after you try something once or twice, you say, 'Check! Done!'"

"Austin, remember when we watched the video of Michael Phelps swimming in the Olympics, and we saw him use the same stroke to race in all sorts of different races? Michael is the kind of swimmer who thinks about the strokes he is really good at, and he uses those strokes again and again in different situations, and he wins and wins and wins! Just like Michael used the butterfly stroke to compete in the relay, and he used the butterfly stroke to compete in the 200 meter, and he used the butterfly stroke to compete in the 400 meter, you can use the strategies you know to make *all* of the writing in your folder the best it can be!

MID-WORKSHOP TEACHING   **Spelling with Efficiency**

"Writers, I want to remind you to not just fix up your sentences but also fix up your words! You already know many ways to spell tricky words, using tools in our classroom to find words you need," I reminded, gesturing toward the class word wall, before continuing, "or using strategies to figure out a way to solve it the best you can." I stood beside a spelling strategy chart to remind children to recall this repertoire.

"Of course, there are words you'll just know how to spell in a snap, because you use them all the time when you write or read them all the time in your books! But some words you'll need to solve, using all you know about how words work, stretching and hearing each part, using words you know to spell a word you need, or trying it a few ways to decide which looks right. And of course, there are other words that are tricky, but you can find them if you use the room. It's your job as a writer to know what kind of word you are writing. So when you get back to your writing, remember, if a tricky word gets in the way, look it right in eye and decide if it's a *Know It* word, a *Solve It* word, or a *Find It* word. Go!"

"You are the kind of writer who adds extra details to convince your readers, but you are only doing it one time. It's time to be like that swimmer! It's time to practice what you know how to do really well on *all* of your reviews and in *lots* of different places."

A tiny smile crept across Austin's face. "I am good at that," he said. "I can do it all over." Then he started shuffling through his reviews. "Like here, and here."

"So are you game for going back to your folder to find places where you can add details to make your reasons stronger?" When Austin nodded, I said, "Show me where you'll do this." I gave Austin some space to do this inquiry work. As he searched, rereading his reviews, I quickly sketched a strategy card to leave behind as a reminder of this conference, urging him to carry this work forward. It read: "Teach more! Add extra details." Then, on a separate strategy card, I wrote: "Keep going! Try it somewhere else."

Austin had located several places to elaborate in his review. "Terrific!" I congratulated. "Now, let's mark these places with Post-it notes, so you'll remember to keep going across all these parts and in all of these reviews to practice again and again. This will make your reviews even more convincing, but more important, it will help make you a stronger writer!"

Before moving on to another student, I awarded Austin the two strategy cards, explaining how I'd like him to use these as a reminder to not only continue to add detail to his writing but to also remember to practice the strategies he knows across his pieces.

Oral Book Reviews

Share an example of an oral book review. Ask partners to discuss what they notice.

When I called the writers back to the meeting area today, I had cued on the Smart Board a half-minute video clip of a *Reading Rainbow* student book review.

"Writers, I have some very exciting news. In a few short days, you will be ready to publish your book reviews. And what is so cool is that you won't just be holding up your writing for everyone to *see*, you'll get to speak up, too, in a way that really convinces others that they just *have to* read the books you recommend. I want to show you a video clip of a little girl telling her opinion and giving a book review of *Imogene's Antlers*. Let's watch, and then we can talk about what you noticed."

Without further ado, I began the short video clip. After just fifteen seconds, I stopped the video. "Writers, what I want you to do now is to talk to your partner about what you noticed Kimmy doing at the very beginning of her book review talk. Is she doing the things that we talked about the other day, giving a sneak peek without giving too much away?" I gestured toward the "Give a Sneak Peek!" list. "Partner 1, you'll talk first today." I circulated through the meeting area, listening in as students conversed.

Give a Sneak Peek!

- Introduce the characters or topic.
- Explain the situation or share an interesting fact.
- Ask a question.

I reconvened the class to summarize what I had overheard. "Many of you are noticing that Kimmy introduced the book and gave a sneak peek about the main character. She told a little bit about what happened to Angelina, but not too much. She even asked us a question, 'Have you ever seen a girl with antlers?' Well, no, I haven't! I want to keep watching her review, and I already feel like I can't wait to read this book! Let's keep watching and listening to see what she says next." I touched the play arrow on the screen, and we watched the remainder of the clip.

This share will require a bit of preparation, searching for and previewing online student book review videos. (A suggested source is provided on the CD.) Choose one that speaks to you and will engage your students. You might choose to forego one last conference in order to cue up your selected clip.

"Okay, writers, we are going to watch Kimmy's book review one more time. This time, think about what you notice Kimmy including in her review. Does she make you want to read the book? How? We'll talk about what you noticed after we watch." I showed the clip once more.

Elicit and chart a list of ways to give a convincing book review.

I again asked partners to turn and talk. After a few minutes, I called the group back together to share. As students spoke, I jotted their observations on chart paper. "Let's make a list of all of the smart things you are noticing in Kimmy's review. What did you notice? What did Kimmy do to be really convincing?"

"She spoke in an excited voice," said Benjamin. "I can tell that she liked the book. If she didn't like it, she wouldn't be so excited to talk about it. And if Kimmy didn't like the book, I might not like it either."

"That's a great point, Benjamin," I stated. "If you are enthusiastic about your book, others will probably be, too!"

"And she told some of the details of what happened in the book," added Rosa. "Like she said how Imogene used her antlers to hang towels and hold donuts to feed the birds. That was so funny." Laughter erupted.

"Another great idea—sharing a *few* details, not too many. And making sure that the details you share are interesting enough to make your readers want to pick up the book. Anything else anyone wants to add?

"Writers, in just a few days, you'll be publishing your book reviews and sharing your opinions with other people in the school. We will ask visitors to come to our classroom to listen to our reviews. The clip we just watched is from a show called *Reading Rainbow*, and the whole show is about reading and the cool things readers do. Each week, boys and girls share their book reviews by doing book talks. We're going to do some of our own book review talks, and just like you noticed everything Kimmy did in her book review," I gestured toward the list we just made, "you'll incorporate those things into your own book review talks. You will even get to make some book review talks on video! And then we can send them all around the school for others to watch and convince them to read the books we love!"

How to Give a Convincing Review

- Speak in an excited voice.
- Give a sneak peek at the beginning.
- Share a few of the details from the book, but not too many.
- Tell details that you think will make others want to read the book.
- Give a reason why you think people should read the book.

You'll want to use transferable language to restate students' observations. These replicable strategies can be recorded on a chart for children to use as they prepare for final publication.

Review a Review?
Making Sure Reviews Are Brim Full of the Best Work!

IN THIS SESSION, you'll teach students that writers use checklists to make sure that each and every part of their writing is as strong as it can be.

GETTING READY

✔ Enlarged copy of the Opinion Writing Checklist, Grades 1 and 2 (see Connection and Teaching) ⊗

✔ Your own book review, enlarged (see Teaching)

✔ Student copies of the Opinion Writing Checklist, Grades 1 and 2 (see Link) ⊗

COMMON CORE STATE STANDARDS: W.1.1, W.1.5, W.2.1, RI.1.8, RFS.1.4, SL.1.1, L.1.1, L.1.2, L.1.6

T HE PAST SEVERAL WEEKS have focused on the important work of opinion writing. You've watched youngsters find their voice and state opinions in crystal-clear words. You've taught them strategies to support those opinions with reasons that are specific and important. You've assessed student work and noticed the elaboration strategies they are using, from both this unit and previous units. As you look across student folders, you aren't seeing the work of just this unit; you are seeing the work of the workshop from day one through day one-hundred-and-whatever-it-happens-to-be today. Their achievements are reason to celebrate.

Most likely, when you set about the work of planning this unit, you checked on the CCSS goals for opinion writing at this grade, noting that those standards expect that students introduce the topic, state an opinion, supply a reason for the opinion, and provide some sense of closure (Common Core State Standard Writing 1.3). As you've gathered student folders and read their writing, you've realized the work writers have done stands head and shoulders above that goal. We imagine you've witnessed lively debates, listening to youngsters convince their friends why the strawberry smelly sticker is the best sticker in their collection. You've read reviews that give recommendations from where to buy ice cream to which movies you should plan to see Saturday afternoon.

As you read across students' book reviews, you'll likely find yourself developing a deeper understanding of children's thinking around books, characters, and topics. The work you've supported during this unit of study will serve as a building block for the writing that students will continue to do as they move through their academic careers. Those lively voices you heard earlier this month, debating rankings of superheroes or sticker collections, are the same voices that will soon stake claims as essayists, whether it be for college entrance or perhaps to talk back to local government representatives.

Today's work sets up youngsters for tomorrow's celebration, asking writers to return to the Opinion Writing Checklist they've used throughout the unit, checking each item and making final revisions in their reviews. Writers will work independently, as well as with partners, reviewing their book reviews, before choosing one they'd like to use as their published piece. You'll return to the work of Session 12, reminding students that checkups are an important part of staying healthy, pairing with partners to peer edit in a final effort to lift the level of as many pieces as possible.

"The work you've supported during this unit of study will serve as a building block for the writing that students will continue to do as they move through their academic careers."

During today's share session, you'll provide an opportunity for students to rehearse their oral presentations, encouraging writers to speak in clear and engaging ways as they practice aloud for the approaching celebration.

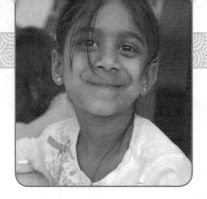

Review a Review?

Making Sure Reviews Are Brim Full of the Best Work!

CONNECTION

Show students a copy of the Opinion Writing Checklist and feign concern that they might not be up for the challenge of using it since it is full of goals for the end of first grade, as well as for second grade.

As the students joined me on the rug to begin workshop, my eyes lingered on the enlarged copy of the Opinion Writing Checklist. My brow was knitted and a slight frown tugged at the corner of my mouth. "Writers, I'm concerned." I sighed. "I'm looking at this checklist made by teachers across the country about what opinion writers need to know how to do by the *end* of first grade." I emphasized the word "end" so they would understand what I was about to challenge them to do. "It's only February, and I'm worried that because it is only February, you won't be able to find each thing in your reviews that strong opinion writers do when they are writing opinions."

There were a couple of concerned faces in the crowd, but mostly I saw smiles and wiggles as eyes were scanning the checklist. There were whispers of "I have that" and "Check! I got it" from the writers around me.

"You still have a few months of first grade left, so there is still time to learn these things," I said, "but since we still have a few days of the opinion writing left to do before our publishing celebration," I pointed to the class's publishing calendar where a bold red circle captured the day our celebration was set to commence, and continued, "I thought perhaps, just maybe, even though it *isn't* the end of first grade and even though you have *lots* of time to learn all this, since we are working as opinion writers right now, maybe you would be up for the challenge of making sure that you are doing *all* of these things to make your book reviews the *best* they can be. Perhaps, even challenging yourself to do some of the things second-graders are expected to do." My voice trailed off, unsure if they were up for such a challenge. "And maybe, just maybe, I can teach you a little secret about how grown-up writers use checklists when they are checking to make sure they did all they can to make their writing the strongest it can be."

I looked to the sea of faces and a resounding "Yes!" filled the room.

"Oh my goodness—so great for you all to be ready to embrace this challenge! Then I'm going to teach you, even though it *isn't* the end of first grade, and certainly not nearly the end of *second grade*! I'm going to use this checklist like grown-up writers. Let's get started!"

Before calling students over to the rug, I asked the class to set up for today's workshop by quickly selecting the book review that revealed their best work. They left their writing on their table, as they wouldn't need it for the minilesson. But by selecting their piece beforehand, they would be able to get started quickly and efficiently when the minilesson was over.

❖ Name the teaching point.

"Today I want to teach you that when writers use checklists to make sure they've made their writing as strong as it can be, they don't just find one place where they did what's on the list, they check each and every part of their writing."

TEACHING

Use the Opinion Writing Checklist to check your own writing.

"Sometimes, even grown-up writers have trouble doing this because it is detailed work, and it doesn't work for every single item on the checklist. There are some items on a checklist that you need to find only one time, but other items, *most of the items*, are things you should be checking for and doing again and again on each page of your writing.

"Watch me try this work right now. Watch and notice how I choose one part of the checklist to use to check my writing. Notice how I check page after page to make sure that I did the item again and again in my writing. Here I go."

Opinion Writing Checklist

	Grade 1	NOT YET	STARTING TO	YES!	Grade 2	NOT YET	STARTING TO	YES!
	Structure				**Structure**			
Overall	I wrote my opinion or my likes and dislikes and said why.	☐	☐	☐	I wrote my opinion or my likes and dislikes and gave reasons for my opinion.	☐	☐	☐
Lead	I wrote a beginning in which I got readers' attention. I named the topic or text I was writing about and gave my opinion.	☐	☐	☐	I wrote a beginning in which I not only gave my opinion, but also set readers up to expect that my writing would try to convince them of it.	☐	☐	☐
Transitions	I said more about my opinion and used words such as *and* and *because*.	☐	☐	☐	I connected parts of my piece using words such as *also, another,* and *because*.	☐	☐	☐
Ending	I wrote an ending for my piece.	☐	☐	☐	I wrote an ending in which I reminded readers of my opinion.	☐	☐	☐
Organization	I wrote a part where I got readers' attention and a part where I said more.	☐	☐	☐	My piece had different parts; I wrote a lot of lines for each part.	☐	☐	☐
	Development				**Development**			
Elaboration	I wrote at least one reason for my opinion.	☐	☐	☐	I wrote at least two reasons and wrote at least a few sentences about each one.	☐	☐	☐
Craft	I used labels and words to give details.	☐	☐	☐	I chose words that would make readers agree with my opinion.	☐	☐	☐
	Language Conventions				**Language Conventions**			
Spelling	I used all I knew about words and chunks of words (*at, op, it,* etc.) to help me spell.	☐	☐	☐	To spell a word, I used what I knew about spelling patterns (*tion, er, ly,* etc.).	☐	☐	☐
	I spelled all the word wall words right and used the word wall to help me spell other words.	☐	☐	☐	I spelled all of the word wall words correctly and used the word wall to help me figure out how to spell other words.	☐	☐	☐

I looked to the checklist and processed aloud my thinking, "Hmm . . . I need to check that 'I wrote my opinion or my likes and dislikes and said why.'" With my finger on the bulleted line of the checklist, I looked back to my writing sitting on the easel and continued, "Let me check for that first. I know I should find my opinion right near the beginning of my writing. So I'll check for it there."

I began rereading the first part of my review to the class:

> **I Am Invited to a Party** is a story about an elephant named Gerald and his friend Piggie. In this story, they are getting ready to go to a party. But there's a big problem! They don't know what kind of party it will be, so they can't decide what to wear! What kind of party will it be? Will Gerald and Piggie figure out what to wear? You'll have to read this book to find out!

I paused, then said, "That's my introduction. No opinion yet. Let me keep reading," and continued,

I Am Invited to a Party is one of the funniest books you'll ever read!

"Hey," I interrupted. "There's my opinion!" I reread the sentence:

I Am Invited to a Party is one of the funniest books you'll ever read!

"That tells my readers what I think about the book. I can check the box because I definitely wrote my opinion." I moved my pen to the first box, marking it with a tiny check.

Think aloud and decide whether you can move on from the bulleted item or whether you need to continue to look through your writing.

"Now I have a decision to make. I must decide if this is something on the list that I just need to check for once or something that I need to make sure I did all the way through my writing." I studied the sea of faces to gauge reactions. "What would you do? Is this something I should do again and again, or is it okay if I move to the next part of the checklist? Give me a 'More, more!' if you think I should keep rereading to keep checking. Give a 'Move, move!' if you think I should move on to the next item on the list. More?" Silence. "Move?"

"Move, move!" the class chanted.

Move on to another item on the checklist, this time rereading and checking for even more examples in your writing.

Moving on to include another bullet to elaborate further on this expectation, "I wrote at least one reason for my opinion." Moving my eyes back to my writing, I continued to check my work, reading the next part of my book review aloud:

Mo Willems is a hilarious author and every page of this story will make you laugh.

"There's one reason!" I remarked. "Should I check the box and *move* to the next item on the checklist, or should I read *more* to challenge myself—checking for at least two reasons, like second-graders do, or even more?" While technically I'd found my one reason, I wanted to take this opportunity to challenge students to consider the possibility of working beyond the checklist. "Should I do more, or should I move on?" Voices, that just a moment before had been confident in their decision making, now faltered. I seized the opportunity to think aloud, modeling the careful revision writers do when using checklists to check their writing.

"Well, even though it says I need at *least* one reason, I'm going to use this checklist like a grown-up writer would use it. I'm going to keep going and reread to check for even more."

Today's minilesson is not about passively recording checks on a list, fulfilling the bare minimum, but about using a checklist to validate and celebrate all children know how to do as writers, while making plans to do even more.

A confident chorus of "More, More!" filled the room, so I continued, "Okay, I need to read more and keep checking my work for reasons. I'll read across my whole review to keep checking." I read on:

Elephant and Piggie dress up in the wackiest outfits!

"There's another reason!" I checked another mark in the box to keep count. "Even though first grade is not yet over, my review shows off things that second-grade opinion writers are expected to do!

"Writers, when you use a checklist, it is important to not just find one place where you did something. You'll want to make your piece the best it can be by checking each and every part of your writing." I continued, highlighting my process to make it that much more explicit, "What I'm doing as a writer is rereading and checking my *whole* piece. Did you see how I did that?" I questioned as thumbs went up to acknowledge understanding.

ACTIVE ENGAGEMENT

Ask students to think about the next item on the checklist and whether they would check one part of their writing for this item and then move on or need to check every part of their writing.

"Now you try it. Make a decision like grown-up writers would when using a checklist—making sure their writing is as strong as it can be, not just finding one place where they did what's on the list but checking each and every part of their writing. They focus their attention on one item from the checklist, then they reread each and every part of their writing and make sure they tried it again and again.

"Let's look back at the checklist." I turned my attention to the checklist and moved my finger to another item on the list, as I read aloud:

I wrote an ending for my piece.

"Writers, think about this item on the checklist for a minute. When you go back to your writing spot and begin checking your writing to make sure that you wrote an ending for your piece, what decision will you make? Is this the kind of item where after you find it one time and 'move, move' onto another item on the list? Or, do you need to use this part of the checklist to reread and do 'more, more' in other parts of your piece? Think a minute, and give me a thumbs up when you have made your decision."

After only a few seconds, thumbs were up and decisions were made.

"Writers, tell your partner what your decision is, and tell your partner *why* that's your decision. Partner 1, will you begin this time?"

I stood and moved to a partnership near the back of the meeting area. I heard Benjamin remark, "I would check one time and move because when you write your writing only needs one ending, just like one beginning—kind of like a story."

As Benjamin explained his decision making, I leaned in and asked, "Benjamin, will you share with the rest of the class the decision you just made?" He nodded, so I asked him to join me at the front of the room.

"Writers, Benjamin made a decision about how he would use this item on the checklist. Benjamin, will you share your decision and the reason you made your decision with the rest of the class?" I asked.

"I think it's a 'move, move' because it says you need to write an ending. When you write a review or a story, you write one ending to end it," he went on to explain.

LINK

Send students off with copies of the Opinion Writing Checklist, Grades 1 and 2, and remind them to check every part of their writing for the items on the list.

"As you go off today, and anytime you are using a checklist to revise your writing, I want to remind you to not just check one place where you did what's on the list but instead to check each and every part of your writing. Then, you can make plans for the work you'll need to do to revise, finding places to do even more to convince your readers. This way, you can make sure you've made your writing as strong as it can be! I have copies of the Opinion Writing Checklist for each of you, so that you can use it the same way that I did, going through each item on the list as you reread the writing you selected for publication."

Using Special Print to Emphasize Words and Phrases
Preparing for Publication

I GATHERED A GROUP OF WRITERS ON THE RUG. Each student had taken out the book review they were planning to publish, placing it on top of their folder. I had a copy of my Elephant and Piggie book review on the easel that now looked like this:

I Am Invited to a Party is a story about an elephant named Gerald and his friend Piggie. In this story, they are getting ready to go to a party. But there's a BIG problem! They don't know what kind

of party it will be, so they can't decide what to wear! What kind of party will it be? Will Gerald and Piggie figure out what to wear? You'll have to <u>read this book to find out</u>!

I began, "Writers, there are many ways writers get ready to publish their writing. One way is to think about words or phrases that you want to stand out to make sure readers pay special attention to them. You can use bold text to make those words

---

MID-WORKSHOP TEACHING   **Sharing the Strategies from Small-Group Work: Using Special Print for Emphasis**

"I need to stop you for a moment, class," I said, and waited for pens to go down and eyes to come up. "I was just working with this table of writers, and they are remembering how as information writers they had ways to make parts of their writing stand out on the page. This group of writers did the same thing in their reviews! Look," I said, and I held Tony's review in the air, pointing out places where he'd gone through and styled several words in boldface for emphasis.

"Tony made important parts stand out on his page by using bold letters. The words and phrases that he wanted to make sure his readers read with emphasis he went over with his pen and made them bold. I bet you might find places to try this, too." (See Figure 17–1.)

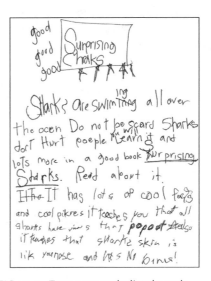

FIG. 17–1   Tony uses underlined words and bold print in his book review to grab readers' attention.

Sharks are swimming all over the ocean. Do not be scared. Sharks don't hurt people. You will learn it and lots more in a good book, <u>Surprising Sharks</u>. Read about it. It has lots of cool facts and cool pictures. It teaches you that all sharks have jaws that POP OUT. Also it teaches that sharks' skin is like your nose and has no bones!

(continues)

I waited a moment, then continued, "Aubrey got her writing ready to publish by going back and underlining important words and phrases in her review. Underlined words or phrases make readers pay special attention to what they are reading. You could do that work, too!" (See Figure 17–2.)

> Big Al is a big fish with <u>a big problem</u>. <u>No friends</u>. Big Al is nice but he's so scary to other fish so other fish swim away from him. Happy ending books are my <u>favorite</u>. If you like happy endings you should go read Big Al. Go read it now, will you now?
>
> Yoshi wrote Big Al and he is a good author. If you <u>never read a Yoshi book</u> why not? <u>You should</u>. Big Al is a Yoshi book and you will like it more than other books!

"Writers, take a moment right now to make important words or phrases stand out in your review. You can use bold print or underline some words or phrases to make readers pay special attention to those parts."

As the class set forth doing the work of making their review ready for publishing, I moved about from writer to writer and publicly exclaimed when I saw a writer trying one of the moves taught, but also naming and acknowledging other ways they were trying to make parts of their review stand out to readers.

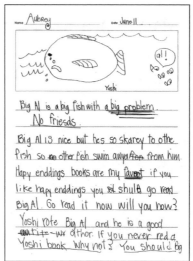

FIG. 17–2 Aubrey's book review uses underlined words and phrases to make the more important parts stand out.

stand out on the page, like I did here," I said, pointing to the place where I'd boldly printed the word "big."

"You can underline certain words or phrases that you want your readers to pay special attention to as they read your review. Look at how I did that in my review. The underline makes readers pay special attention to this phrase."

I went on to include a final option, "You can also use exclamation marks to make parts of your review stand out to readers. Like I did here," gesturing toward the example from my own writing. "That mark tells readers to get excited as they read!"

"You've used these strategies before as information writers, but right now let's try this work in our reviews to get them ready to publish. Reread your review to decide which words or phrases should stand out."

I briskly moved from student to student, coaching writers as they explored ways to make parts of their writing stand out. I focused my attention on making sure that once writers had revised to add bold print, underlines, or exclamation points, they reread their piece with emphasis on the word or phrase, reflecting on their decisions.

Reading and Rehearsing
Paying Attention to Punctuation to Read with Expression

Have students rehearse their oral presentations for the celebration. Remind them to pay attention to punctuation when they are speaking.

"Writers, you worked hard today to get your book reviews ready to publish. Remember, tomorrow we'll have a celebration! We are going to give book talks to other people in the school. Just like singers and dancers have rehearsals before the big show, readers have rehearsals before they read their pieces aloud. They make sure to read their pieces clearly and to pay close attention to punctuation marks to change their voices in special ways.

"Let's practice this work with partners. Read your reviews like you're on *Reading Rainbow*, making sure to stop at punctuation marks and making sure to change your voice when you come to a part that has bold or underlined words. This way, those parts will not just stand out on the page, they'll also stand out as we read out loud. Ready, set, rehearse!"

This rehearsal not only gives kids an opportunity to prepare for the celebration, but it also reinforces students' understanding of the role punctuation and special print has in phrasing and reading expression.

Book Review Talks
A Reading Rainbow–Style Celebration

ear Teachers,

You've reached the end of the unit, and as you reflect on all that you and your writers have accomplished over the past weeks, we hope you'll think about the width and breadth of the unit. Since the purpose of this unit is writing to convince an audience, we feel it is important that others hear your students' voices, helping their words reach ears outside your classroom community. After all, if you want to persuade, your opinions will need to be heard!

You'll find that today's session is presented as a letter with one possibility for how your celebration may unfold. We know that you will make the decision of how and in what exciting ways you'll celebrate all your children have done as opinion writers.

Since this is a celebration for the end of the unit, you'll likely decide to plan one that incorporates students both speaking and listening, asking children to deliver book review talks to one another, and then to present their recommendations to visitors, reading their reviews aloud with a focus on fluency and intonation. Our suggestion is that you set up a *Reading Rainbow* set of some sort. It need not be especially extravagant—after all, the original set featured a child at a table, holding a book. Simple! We suggest you invite people outside your immediate classroom community, perhaps family members, or a class of fifth-graders, or kindergartners, or other adults from the school. You may want to solicit some family member volunteers to videotape your students as they give their book reviews, or create your own *Reading Rainbow* program to be shared throughout the larger school community, allowing the work your writers have done across this unit to live on long after the final celebration.

COMMON CORE STATE STANDARDS: W.1.1, W.1.2, W.1.6, RFS.1.4, SL.1.1, SL.1.4, SL.1.6, L.1.1, L.1.2

PREPARATION

Yesterday's session had students using checklists to revise their book reviews in careful and methodical ways, asking questions of themselves, making decisions and checking across their pieces, before moving forward. Our hope is that students are now reading the entire body of their review, taking greater care in the assessments they make of their writing.

You will likely begin today with a giant round of applause to acknowledge all that your writers have done from Day One until now. As you remind them of the fun that is about to come, when they deliver book review talks to visiting guests, you'll ask them to call upon the *Reading Rainbow* book reviews they watched just a couple of days ago. It may be that you play an additional clip during today's connection and allow your writers to turn and talk about all they noticed about the readers' delivery.

It may prove helpful to divide the class into small groups, perhaps separating writing partners, and ask that they meet in these groups to rehearse their reviews aloud, once more. You'll prompt the groups to offer feedback to one another after each reading and to go through their review again and again, as needed.

Meanwhile, you'll want to conduct very quick check-in conferences to make sure children are speaking clearly and listening to each other's pieces. You'll guide writers to use a friendly, talking-right-to-the-listener voice, perhaps with body language or simple gestures to captivate their audience. You may even take moments to briefly model for small groups how you sound when you are delivering a book review talk, offering students time to contrast how book review talks sound different than reading. Don't shy away from replaying quick clips from the *Reading Rainbow* reviews you've downloaded the last few days.

You might ask that children hold onto a physical copy of the book they have reviewed, presenting it to their audience as they deliver their recommendation. Others, instead, might hold up their own cover designs, depicting the characters or the topic along with the title and author's name. Of course, you might also provide students with an opportunity to search for the book on the Internet and print an image of the cover to use when presenting their review.

THE CELEBRATION
A *Reading Rainbow* Fair

As guests arrive, ask that students take a seat at an assigned spot around the classroom, perhaps sitting behind a long row of desks, or on one of many chairs arranged in a crescent shape in the classroom library. However you decide to lay out these stations, you'll want to cluster students around the room in a way that allows guests to listen to a number of reviews as they move across the classroom. Students will hold onto their published reviews, along with the books or cover pages, as they welcome their audience.

If your audience contains family members, simply ask them to join their child. If you have guests from the school as your visitors, quickly ask them to spread across the groups to keep the numbers fairly even. Group members, students, and visitors alike will rotate together to each station.

You might voice over to students that even though they are reading from their review, they'll want to make sure they are reading as though they are talking, using a friendly and persuasive voice. Remind them, gently, that reviews are friendly, not bossy, and that when writers talk about their opinions, they want to talk about them in ways that convince others to agree.

As a cherry on top, ask volunteers to assist you in recording short video clips of the children delivering their *Reading Rainbow* book reviews. Once downloaded onto the computer, you may choose to make a link for parents, or the larger school community, to access and watch students talking about and reviewing books.

Have fun!

Congratulations,

Lucy, Celena, and Liz

STUDENTS' PUBLISHED REVIEWS

I love Tale of Despereaux because it is an action story and you should ask your teacher to read it to you for read aloud and my teacher read it and it was a good story. One reason I love the story is because the characters are brave and Despereaux is brave even though he is little and his father says he is not good but he is wrong and Despereaux is a little mouse but he is brave. It is so good because Despereaux doesn't act like his brother or sister mice. He can read and he loves music. And he talks like people talk. You will love Despereaux when you read this book too and you will even love the bad rat a little I think because he is a bad rat but he is a sad rat. Pea is a princess and Despereaux loves her. There is also a bad rat that is sad. Fern is a girl that is bad but not bad. That is the adventure in this book. Read it and you will like it.

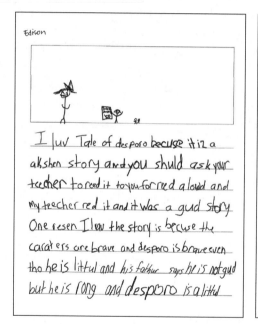

FIG. 18–1   Edison's published book review gives a sneak peek summary without telling readers too much.

Surprising Sharks is the best shark book you will ever read!! Read it right away because it has the coolest pictures in it. Here are some facts from Surprising Sharks but not all the facts because you should read it to learn more. Dwarf Lantern sharks light up because their organs have light up things. Some sharks have saw shapes for heads or some have hammer shapes for heads. Some sharks eat shrimp. Sand sharks babies eat other babies inside the mother sack inside the mother stomach. A lot of sharks get killed by people to make lipstick. Bad! Don't kill a shark!! Did you like those facts? You will like Surprising Sharks. There is even more information in that book. Read it. Read it. Read it right now. Go to the library. Go to Barnes and Noble. Read it. You might even buy it to keep.

Has your mom made you wear something you hate? The puppy in this book has to wear a bow. She hates it! She tries to take it off but . . .

I'm not telling!

Read this book and you will find out. If you need a tip where to find it, come to Mrs. Nealy's room. It's in the double green dot basket. Double green dot means H book so be an H reader or I will read it to you and we will laugh.

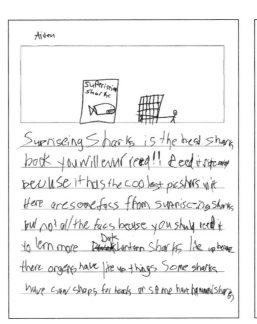
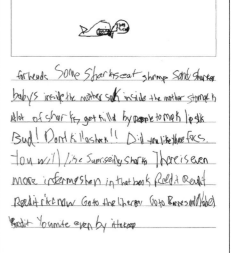

FIG. 18–2   Aiden's published book review includes a catchy introduction and a conclusion that urges readers to act fast.

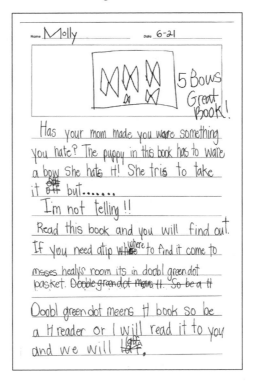

FIG. 18–3   Molly's published book review compels readers with a sneak peek summary that sparks curiosity.